RALPH CREASMAN studied at the Art Institute of Chicago, Peabody College, Nashville, and the New School for Social Research. His work has appeared in national magazines, and he has illustrated several children's books. Mr. Creasman, a Chicago freelance artist, divides his time between his art work and research on primitive cultures.

CONQUISTADOR
WITHOUT SWORD

CONQUISTADOR

WITHOUT

The Life of
Roque González, S.J.

Loyola University Press

SWORD

C. J. McNaspy, S.J.

© 1984 C.J. McNaspy, S.J.
Printed in the United States of America.

Library of Congress Cataloging in Publication Data

McNaspy, C. J. (Clement J.), 1915-
    Conquistador without sword.

1. González de Santa Cruz, Roque, 1576-1628.
2. Guarani Indians—Missions.
3. Indians of South America—Paraguay—Missions.
4. Jesuits—Paraguay— Biography.
5. Missionaries—Paraguay— Biography. I. Title.

F2684.G643M36   1984
266'.2'0924 [B]   84-12200
ISBN 0-8294-0455-4

Illustrated by Ralph Creasman

Book design by Carol Tornatore

Contents

PREFACE

EXCEPT for history buffs, most readers whose native language is not Spanish would be hard pressed if asked to name five conquistadors. Cortés, of course, quickly pops into mind, especially if one happens to be from North America, with Pizarro a close second. Ponce de León, De Soto, and Cabeza de Vaca might also come to mind, the last being almost a folk hero to Americans from the Southwest.

But even Southwesterners may not recall de Vaca's South American feats, such as his crossing from the coast of Brazil to what is now Paraguay. To the list of almost legendary explorers of the Southern Cone—the vast La Plata area including Argentina, Chile, Uruguay, and Paraguay—would be added Diego de Almagro, Pedro de Mendoza, Vasco Nuñez de Balboa, Juan Díaz de Solís, Domingo Martínez de Irala, and other stalwarts memorialized in South America.

1

The non-historian may be even less aware of a different kind of "conquest" that was going on at the same time as the pursuit of empire and *El Dorado*. Giants no less intrepid, but bearing the cross rather than the sword, were giving their lives in what became known as the Spiritual Conquest. These men struggled and died to bring the Gospel to native Americans, not to take gold or anything else from them. The first of these were men of the cloth, principally Franciscans, Dominicans, Mercedarians, and diocesan priests.

In the middle of the sixteenth century, the newly founded Society of Jesus, or Jesuits, enthusiastically joined the enterprise. One of them, Antonio Ruiz de Montoya, left us an important book called precisely *Spiritual Conquest*, which I have just translated into English and expect to publish in 1985, the 400th anniversary of his birth.

Montoya's slightly older contemporary, Roque González de Santa Cruz, is better known internationally, since he died a martyr and has been solemnly declared Blessed

2

by the Roman Catholic Church. As this is being written, the government of Paraguay, as well as all the Catholic bishops of Paraguay, Argentina, Uruguay, and South Brazil have petitioned the pope to canonize Blessed Roque, to officially declare him a saint.

Both Roque González and Ruiz de Montoya were American-born; Roque being a native of Asunción and Montoya of Lima, the vice-regal capital of all South America. Both men, with hundreds of others, can fittingly be called "Conquistadors without Swords."

It so happens that Roque, when declared Blessed by Pope Pius XI on January 25, 1934, was the first martyr so named of those born and killed in Spanish America. This is not to say that he was America's first martyr. As early as 1516, the Franciscan missioner Fernando Salcedo, together with two companions, was killed by cannibal Caribs in the Antilles. In 1541 the Dominican Bishop Vicente Valverde was martyred at Guayaquil, Ecuador; while Franciscan Juan de Padilla gave his life in or near Texas, the first martyr of present-day North America. And

3

between 1549 and 1597, Franciscans, Dominicans, and Jesuits attempting to evangelize Florida were also slaughtered. The list could go on and on.

Several circumstances, however, make the case of Roque González exceptional. One is the fact that he was not a missioner sent from Europe, but was born in America. As English historian Herbert Thurston observed, Roque is "the first beatified martyr of Spanish America." Note the careful qualifications; for Jean de Brébeuf, Isaac Jogues, and their Jesuit confrères were canonized in 1930; but they were French-born. The popular Rose of Lima was canonized as early as April 12, 1671, and there were other Spanish American non-martyred saints. Furthermore, the Mexican San Felipe de las Casas died a martyr in 1597, but in Nagasaki, Japan.

A surprising detail that makes Roque's case unusual is the abundance of available material regarding his life and death. While he was certainly surrounded with legends, his actual accomplishments were so heroic that almost every major event in his life is richly documented. Again Herbert Thurston points out that official investigations with a view to his beatification began less than five months after his death. This is in striking contrast to the cases of more famous saints, like Teresa of Avila, in whose case investigations began thirteen years after her death, or Ignatius of Loyola, thirty-nine years after his death.

In some ways, the abundance of information facilitates a biographer's task. For how many historical personalities do we possess 850 pages of eye-witness testimony? At times, while digging through such a mass of material, I have sighed for less, not more material, especially since redundancy abounds. At the same time I have been immeasurably helped by J. M. Blanco's *Historia Documentada* (Amorrortu, Buenos Aires, 1929), which makes the material a bit more manageable in just over 740 pages. There is also his briefer 161-page biography *Los Mártires del Caaró e Yjuhí* (Surgo, Buenos Aires, 1931).

Of the twenty-six missioners who died violent deaths during the evangelization of the Paraguay area, two other Jesuits were companions of Roque during his last days on earth and shared in his martyrdom. Spanish-born Alonso Rodríguez, aged twenty-nine, was killed just minutes after Roque; while Juan del Castillo, age thirty-four, died two days later. The three were beatified together and will presumably be declared saints at the same time. Comparatively little is known of the lives of these two younger missioners except for the climactic moments, and it is understandable that local interest, save in their home towns of Zamora and Cuenca in Spain, can hardly match that awarded Roque. Accordingly, if this brief biography touches on them only peripherally, my intention is not to belittle their heroism. This biographer, being limited in his source materials and for weightier reasons as well, cannot presume to be the final artiber of spiritual greatness.

In Latin America especially, what is

sometimes loosely called "liberation theology" has been more than a vogue for some time. One can hardly live in Latin America without sensing, sometimes with rage, the need for drastic socioeconomic reforms. Roque González was at least as sensitive to injustices and inequities in his day as was Archbishop Oscar Romero, the martyr of our own time. See James Brockman's authoritative biography, *The Word Remains*, Orbis, 1982.

I was inclined to title this biography *Liberator Without a Sword*, since Roque Gonzáles did liberate thousands of Guaraní Indians from his fellow creoles (Spaniards born in America) and even from his closest relatives. But the term *liberator* is redolent rather of the early nineteenth century, and especially of Simón Bolívar, whose bicentennial has just been celebrated and who is popularly known as *El Liberador*.

Roque, on the other hand, belonged to a much earlier generation, that of the *Conquistadores*, or perhaps more exactly that of the colonizers, who were conquistadors in their own way. Being seminomadic, the Guaraní Indians and other indigenous Americans east of the Andes were to become a different sort of prey for rapacious Europeans. Where there were mines to work, as in Bolivia, the Indians could be and often were forced laborers—this was the *mita* system. Though theoretically this system demanded work for only part of the year, it easily led to abuses and frightful exploitation; even if it was not, as many historians believe, as harsh as the "debt peonage" that followed South American independence.

In any case, the Spanish colonists were disinclined to do heavy manual labor themselves, preferring to conquer natives and force them to do what tradition judged to be below the dignity of caballeros. Broader in its implication and actually more common in the Paraguay area was the *encomienda* system, explained in an appendix, against which Roque and other Jesuits in the reductions consistently struggled.

While Roque does not refer to himself as a conquistador, he describes his task as that of "preaching our holy faith, as the Apostles did, and not with the sword." Yet, in the rhetoric of the day, this entire apostolic enterprise was thought of as a "spiritual conquest." It should be noted that the Spanish verb *conquistar* has a connotation somewhat wider than our English *conquer*. In Spanish it often means, rather, to "win over" both literally and metaphorically. Even today I have heard young Paraguayans exclaim: *Ella me conquistó* ("she really won me over!"), in all innocence. The same expression is often used to describe a song or a flower or a sunset or Iguazu Falls as "conquering" them. In this more humane sense, Roque can rightly be called a conquistador.

Were I to thank here all my Jesuit confreres who helped make this small book possible, the list would turn into an unseemly litany. I feel most indebted to Jesús Montero Tirado and Daniel A. Flaherty for pressing me to do it in both Spanish and English, to Eugene

Geinzer and Alberto Luna for their cartography, to Donald J. Martin for pointing out several of Herbert Thurston's surprising discoveries, to José María Blanch for a number of photographs, and to George Lane for seeing the English version into print.

C. J. McNaspy, S.J.
Asunción, Paraguay
1984

BEGINNINGS

The Setting

TUCKED in between the vast expanses of Brazil and Argentina on the map of South America, Paraguay appears rather small, something like Uruguay, with which it is sometimes confused by northerners. With few more than three million inhabitants, most of them living in deep poverty by United States standards, Paraguay is certainly no major power in the world of nations.

When Roque González de Santa Cruz was born in Asunción, some time in 1576, the place was less than forty years old as a settlement and even less as the capital of the Paraguay area. A glance at the map suggests that two other cities would have been better suited to serve as the capital of the area, Buenos Aires or Montevideo, both of which are strategically located as ports linking Spain with the entire La Plata area.

13

Yet Montevideo was not founded, even
as a modest fort, until 1717; while Buenos
Aires, though started in 1536 by gold-seeking
Pedro de Mendoza, was destroyed by raid-
ing Indians in 1541. Its inhabitants then re-
settled in Asunción, a safer place. But even
after its second start, Buenos Aires remained
under the civil administration of Asunción
until 1617, and only received its own bishop
as late as 1620.

Conquistadors and other explorers had
opened up the huge river system: the Paraná, Paraguay, and Uruguay, sources of
LaPlata. Juan Díaz de Solís came as early as
1516, Magellan in 1520, Alejo García in 1524,
Sebastian Cabot in 1526-27, and Juan de Ay-
olas at about the same time. Asunción was
founded as a fort under Juan de Salazar and
Pedro de Mendoza on August 15, 1537, the
feast of the Assumption of Mary into heaven;
hence, Asunción. Domingo Martínez de Irala
was elected governor by the colonists, and
in 1541 he set up the first *cabildo*, municipal
council, in all America.

The lifetime of Roque González, 1576-

1628, must be seen against the backdrop of an important transition in Asunción, that from a base of operations for conquistadors to a colony—from dreams of gold hunters to the more sober reality of survival and subsistence. The entire La Plata Basin—including, as we have seen, most of Argentina, all of Paraguay, and the southern part of modern Brazil—was undergoing political, economic, social, and cultural changes. Historian Rafael Eladio Velázquez, who has studied the epoch closely, points out that between 1576, when Roque González was born, and 1628, when he died, the entire area had changed substantially.

Paraguay was already a diocese, created in 1547 with Asunción as the bishop's see or headquarters. Its cathedral was built the following year, a very modest structure situated near the present nineteenth-century building. The first bishop of Asunción, Juan de Barrios, a Franciscan, died before he ever arrived there. His successor, Pedro Fernándes de la Torre, also a Franciscan, was appointed in 1556; but little is known of him.

The third bishop, yet another Franciscan,
Juan del Campo, was appointed and even
inaugurated on February 11, 1575; but he
died several days before the confirming pa-
pal document arrived from Rome. It is hard
for us to conceive the difficulties which were
caused by sheer distance in this early period.
Under the best of conditions, a transatlantic
journey took three months or more, and conditions were seldom ideal. In fact, until the
twentieth century Paraguayan church history remained exceptionally spotty.

The next two bishops were both members of the Augustinian order, Luis López
Solís and Juan de Almaraz; but neither of
them ever reached Asunción. Indeed, at the
time of Roque's birth in 1576, Paraguay had
no bishop at all. Nor was this exceptional.
As the late Angel Acha Duarte writes in his
account of the bishops of Paraguay, "of the
first forty bishops named by Rome, only
twenty ever reached Paraguay to be installed
in their cathedral!"

Nevertheless, religious life proved
strong, thanks largely to the missionaries of

16

the various religious orders. Many were to die violent deaths while in service. In 1536 or 1537, as Asunción was being founded, a priest from one of the orders is known to have been slaughtered by the Agaces Indians, though neither his name nor that of his order is documented. Some writers believe that he was a Franciscan, but documents published in 1971 by Eudoxio de J. Palacio suggest that he was Juan de Almasia, a member of the Mercedarian order. In any case, we know that Franciscans and Mercedarians were among the first priests in the Paraguay area, as well as a number of diocesan priests, some years before the Jesuits came.

In February, 1575, a year before Roque's birth, twenty-two Franciscan friars arrived, among them two missionary giants, Alonso de San Buenaventura and Luis de Bolaños. The latter especially played a major role in Paraguayan religious life as a missioner and also as the translator of a catechism prepared by the Third Provincial Council of Lima in 1582-83. The catechism was approved five years later by Pope Sixtus V.

17

This missionary instrument, translated into Guaraní—which is still the first or second language of Paraguayans today—proved to be of major importance. Further, Luis de Bolaños composed a basic grammar and vocabulary of the Guaraní language, a pioneer work at the time. Unfortunately, neither of these works survives, though the Bolaños' translation of the Lord's Prayer has been preserved. While this original translation is not the standard Guaraní version in use today, when I read it to an unlettered person and asked whether she understood it, she replied without hesitation: "Sure, it's the Our Father."

Luis de Bolaños became a close friend, helper, and admirer of Roque González. The first Jesuit superior of the area, Diego de Torres Bollo, described Bolaños as "a great apostle and the person who did most for the teaching of the Indian language, since he reduced it to grammar and translated into it the catechism as well as a manual for confessions and sermons." Bolaños died in Buenos Aires on October 11, 1629, just eight days

after he gave solemn witness to the martyrdom and virtues of Roque González during
the canonical "process" that led to his beatification. Bolaños was one of the makers of
church history in this part of the world, and
one suspects that had he too died as a martyr. If he had been a native-born Paraguayan,
he would very likely be as much venerated
here as is Roque.

So it was that even without a resident
bishop in Paraguay, religious life was thriv-
ing at the time of Roque's birth. In addition
to the Franciscans and Mercedarians, the cathedral had its cabildo with dean, archdea-
con, and three canons. The canons were cler-
ics specifically assigned to chant the Divine
Office, the official prayer of the Church. In
fact, during the first two decades of the Spanish presence, we note a growing number of
secular clergy working in Paraguay. Still,
since surviving documents are so scarce, we
know of no Paraguayan ordained a priest
until 1595; the first was Rodrigo Ortiz Melgarejo.

Another aspect of Paraguayan society

essential to its history almost from the beginning to the present day is the fact of *mestizaje*, the blending of Spanish with indigenous blood. An order of King Philip IV decreed that in Paraguay the mixed-blood descendants of the conquistadors "have always been considered sons of Spaniards and treated with the privileges and exemptions of the same." Even today most Paraguayans are, or proudly claim to be, mestizos.

Yet another relevant fact, especially in Roque's life, was the arrival of the Jesuits in Paraguay. Obviously none of them were present at the founding of Asunción in 1537, since the order did not yet officially exist. While it had been founded by Ignatius of Loyola on August 15, 1534, exactly three years before Asunción, it was not officially approved by Pope Paul III until September 27, 1540, when the city was three years old.

Among the first Jesuits was Francis Xavier, who was soon to be the first Jesuit foreign missioner, Apostle of Asia, and a living symbol of the constant Jesuit thrust as a missionary order. Even while Xavier was pioneering in Asia, Ignatius sent a team of six Jesuits to America. Their leader was Manuel de Nóbrega, who participated in the founding of Salvador (Bahía) on March 29, 1549, the first capital of Brazil. His statue stands in the central plaza there. With Nóbrega came Leonardo Nunes, who was later to play a part in the Paraguayan mission, too. In the following year, 1550, four other Jesuits reached Brazil, their leader being Blessed José de Anchieta, a founder of the city of São Paulo. His statue stands in the main plaza there near the cathedral of that metropolis. São Paulo was to play an important, if ironical, role in the work of the Jesuits in Paraguay, as we shall see.

Somewhat later, on October 6, 1566, Pedro Martínez, a Spanish Jesuit missioner working in Florida, would be the first Jesuit martyr of North America. And in the following year, 1567, the first Jesuits arrived in Peru. From there they spread to present-day Bolivia and Chile; and in 1585, answering the call of Fray Francisco de Victoria, bishop of Tucumán, several Jesuits went to Argentina, which was then part of Paraguay.

The first three Jesuits to arrive in Asunción came by way of Brazil, in 1588. They were an international team including the Portuguese Manuel Ortega (1560-1622), a Catalonian, Juan Saloni (1540-1599), and an Irishman, Thomas Fields (1549-1625). It is hardly fanciful to see in this international trio a foreshadowing of the Jesuits who were eventually to come from thirty-one different countries to work in the missions of Paraguay. More will be said of these Jesuit Reductions in connection with Roque González' pioneer work.

One aspect of this giant missionary venture known as the Reductions that has received little if any attention may be cited here, the surprising number of native-born Paraguayan Jesuits like Roque who participated in them. Thanks to the research of Hugo Storni, we now have a complete catalog of the 1571 men who belonged to the Jesuit Province of Paraguay before the expulsion of the order in 1767-68. Of these, 83 were born in Asunción. In fact, Asunción gave more Jesuits to the province before they were expelled than did any other city, including Madrid, Seville, Barcelona, or Buenos Aires.

While the Storni catalog does not include data on family relationships, the names of these early Paraguayan Jesuits ring a familiar bell here in Paraguay even today. For example, there were six Jesuits named Yegros, still a renowned Paraguayan family, which includes a recently ordained bishop. There were several others named Silva, Insaurralde, Rojas, Caballero, Ortiz, and Benítez—names of present-day Paraguayan Jesuits. Asunción boasts of being the "Mother of Cities,"since Buenos Aires and other cities were founded or refounded from it. It may also appropriately be called the "Mother of Jesuits" with at least as much right.

The word "Paraguay" had already appeared in Jesuit documents during the lifetime of Ignatius of Loyola, 1491-1556. As early as June 29, 1552, Leonardo Nunes wrote his religious superior, Manuel da Nóbrega advising him that several Spaniards had arrived from Paraguay and reported on the spiritual needs of the people there. He assured Nóbrega that it would be very beneficial to have Jesuit missioners there, both among the Spaniards and, even more so, among the native people.

In fact, Ignatius himself wrote shortly before he died on July 31, 1556: "We have word from Brazil that our men have been in communication with those in the Capitalía of São Vicente (near São Paulo) from a Spanish city called Paraguay [sic], in the Rio Plata area, 150 leagues [roughly 450 miles] from the house of those men. They are very urgently petitioning Father Nóbrega and promise to do everything he might ask, since people are needed to teach not only Indians but Spaniards as well."

During its first years, the Jesuit mission in Paraguay underwent many ups and downs. It served especially as a base from which Jesuits went out to work among the natives. In 1594 the great missioner Juan Romero (1560-1630) arrived in Asunción. He encouraged the other missioners and asked for more workers, insisting that "this town is most important, in fact, one of the most important that the Society could serve." Ten years later, when it seemed that Jesuits were about to withdraw from the mission, Romero protested to the superior general in Rome: "Our Society is losing a great harvest by leaving Paraguay. It is the harvest most in need, as I understand, in all the Indies." Happily the mission was not abandoned.

In the following year, 1605, Marciel de Lorenzana (1565-1632) and José Cataldini (1571-1653) came to Asunción. Two years later, the arrival of the superior Diego de Torres Bollo (1551-1638) meant, as Hugo Storni puts it, "the true foundation of the Jesuit province of Paraguay; and two years later the college of Asunción produced its most valued result, the famed Guaraní Reductions." In this particular chapter of mission history Roque González de Santa Cruz would play a central role.

Family and Boyhood

ROQUE was born in Asunción, "the legitimate son of elderly Bartolomé González de Villaverde and María de Santa Cruz," as we read in the contemporary documents. Curiously, these documents do not mention the exact date of his birth or baptism. We are thus in the same situation as in the case of Ignatius of Loyola, not to mention countless other historical personages whose baptismal or birth records have disappeared.

Despite this lack—again as in the case of St. Ignatius—we are richly informed about Roque's family and background. Thanks in great part to painstaking research done by the Argentine historian Ricardo de Lafuente Machain, we have, in fact, a rather exceptional amount of information regarding Roque's immediate family. This was published in *Los parientes del Beato Roque González de Santa Cruz,* Buenos Aires, 1934.

Roque's father, Bartolomé, was born in the city of León, Spain. He came to America in the expedition of Pedro de Mendoza. During political struggles between partisans of Mendoza and Domingo de Irala, Bartolomé returned to Spain in April, 1539, in the capacity of a "royal scribe."

When Bartolomé was returning to South America, his flotilla's pilot lost his way in the maze of rivers and sailed up the Uruguay, convinced that he was on the Paraná. When convinced of his error, the pilot headed back to the mouth of La Plata and finally discovered the Paraná. The adventures were still not over, however, since a storm blew up and scattered the ships. This made the fleet an easy prey to Indians, who slaughtered or wounded several of the expeditionaries.

The expeditionaries finally reached Asunción December 20, 1542, where they found a town transformed. The fairly primitive fort they had left was well on its way to becoming a capital city. In the meantime, Buenos Aires had been destroyed and its inhabitants had moved to Asunción. The arrival of Cabeza de Vaca and his troops earlier that year, in March, 1542, meant a considerable increase of population; in the words of a contemporary document, "not only in quantity but also in quality."

A month and a half after Bartolomé's return, an accidental fire on February 3, 1543, led to the construction of new houses with fairly spacious patios on larger plots of land. According to the chronicler Rui Díaz de Guzmán, Asunción was "more than a league [roughly three miles] long and a mile wide." The main plaza was extensive and was faced by several churches, the principal one occupying the spot where the fortress had been. Other churches mentioned in documents were La Encarnación, la Merced, Santa Lucia, San Sebastián, and San Blas (for Indians). In addition there were several hermitages. Altogether, Asunción was a city of some consequence.

Urbanization, however, did not heal the rivalries and enmities transplanted from Spain to America, some of them were family vendettas, others were regional. Another factor, for better and for worse, in the social structure of Asunción, was the surprisingly young age of many of the captains and other leaders. For example, Alonso Riquelme was only 17 years old, while Francisco Ortiz de Vergara was a year younger. Both family names are still common in Asunción, and it is quite possible that these two young men enjoyed an enormous progeny.

During the night of St. Mark's feast, April 25, 1544, a riot broke out against governor Cabeza de Vaca, the famous conquistador. He was forthwith imprisoned. Roque's father, Bartolomé, "mounted a bench to read out loud so that all could understand what a traitorous tyrant" the governor was. These words are from a manifesto of the revolutionary movement.

Accusations were hurled from both sides, including charges against Bartolomé González himself. After Cabeza de Vaca was expelled from the region, González was appointed "Scribe of the Cabildo and Regiment of the Province." He was evidently a man of political stature.

At the same time, no document informs us of the date of Bartolomé's marriage or of his death. In 1582 it is stated that "the only scribe is named Bartolomé González, who is over seventy years of age." A document which treats of his daughter's dowry, seven years later, refers to him as deceased.

The life of Roque's mother, María de Santa Cruz, is harder to document, since passenger lists from that time are incomplete and her name appears nowhere. A certain Juan de Santa Cruz, however, is listed among the companions of Pedro de Mendoza. And a Pedro de Santa Cruz wrote the proclamation of Juan de Salazar, after the departure of Cabeza de Vaca, offering pardon to all those who had been involved in the uprising. These two men may have been relatives of María. Lafuente Machain, however, states that the only Santa Cruz certainly related to Roque's mother was Blas de Santa Cruz, a conquistador then living in the city of Concepción del Bermejo.

Roque was either the youngest or one of the youngest of ten children born to Don Bartolomé and Doña María. Outstanding among his siblings was Francisco, born in 1560, and thus sixteen years older than

Roque. He was clearly a man of parts and held important posts in Asunción and other cities, one of them being Vera (today called Corrientes), Argentina, where he served as alcalde. In Asunción he held the offices of judge, military captain, and alcalde, and twice he served as lieutenant governor.

Francisco also married well, especially after the death of his first wife Juana de Orue y Zárate. His second marriage was to the sister of Hernandarias de Saavedra, one of the most influential men in the Southern Cone at that time. His name will come up a number of times in the life history of Roque.

Another brother of Roque was called Diego. He held the position relinquished by his father as scribe of the cabildo and several other important civil and military posts as well. Yet another brother, José, held a public office with the resounding title of "Guardian of the City's Horses and Pasture Land."

Two other brothers, Gabriel and Mateo, had something to do with church activities, though it is not clear whether they were ordained priests. On the other hand, Pedro

Gonzáles, born about 1572, was surely a priest; and both Bishop Reginaldo de Lizárraga and Governor Marín Negrón refer to him as a model churchman, "of exemplary character, outstanding among the native-born Paraguayans." He served as canon of the cathedral and participated in the synod, or clergy gathering, that was convoked by Benedictine Bishop Cristóbal de Aresti. After Roque's death, Pedro was naturally appointed to celebrate the solemn Mass in the cathedral commemorating his brother.

Roque's sisters, Francisca, María, and Mariana married well, offering considerable dowries as befitted members of a wealthy family. Lafuente Machain has made a study of their many descendants, who are found not only in Paraguay but in several cities of Argentina as well. It is not surprising that here in Asunción one constantly meets people who claim to be related to Roque. A prominent ecclesiastic, in fact, smilingly assured me that "everybody in Asunción is related to Roque González de Santa Cruz!"

Four years before Roque's birth in 1576,

the Franciscan Bishop Pedro Fernández de la Torre died. Though three bishops were chosen and appointed during the ensuing years, none arrived in Asunción until 1584. In that year the Dominican Alonso de Guerra brought with him several confreres and entrusted them with the parish church of La Encarnación. In 1589 the bishop was expelled from his diocese, and Asunción was again without a bishop until 1603.

Roque received his first education, quite naturally, within his family. He probably also attended classes given by Bishop Alonso de Guerra, described by a contemporary as "taught with great care and for the good of the church." He must also have been initiated into Spanish composition, the elements of Latin, and the ABC's of prayer and the spiritual life.

Roque was twelve years old when the Jesuits first came to Asunción. It seems quite likely, according to Hugo Storni, that his spiritual director was Juan Saloni (1540-1594), the first Jesuit superior in the city. Diego de Boroa Bollo, who would later be

the first Jesuit provincial superior, heard
Father Marciel de Lorenzana speak of Roque
as Saloni's "disciple in letters and spiritual
matters."

The older biographers of saints (hagiog-
raphers, as they were called) seemed to re-
lish expanding and elaborating real or ima-
ginary details of their heroes' lives.
Picturesque episodes were generously in-
vented in lieu of authenticated facts. In
Roque's case, however, we are fortunate to
have eyewitnesses who lived close to him,
knew the facts, and under oath presumably
reported them with reasonable accuracy.

One such witness was Gabriel Insaurralde, a sergeant major and royal standard
bearer who later in his life served in what is
now Corrientes, Argentina. Gabriel had
grown up in Asunción with Roque and knew
him as few others did. In 1630, during the
proceedings leading to Roque's beatification,
Gabriel solemnly swore: "He was so great in
virtue that he always talked with other children only of the service of Our Lord, the

34

contempt of worldly things, and the abhorrence of evil."

Even allowing for some rhetorical exaggeration, it is clear from all the evidence that Roque had, even as a child, a strong personality and leadership qualities. In one episode Insaurralde becomes quite specific: "He persuaded this witness and others to go out into the woods and deserted areas with him in order to do penance. For this he read us lives of saints who had done the same in the desert. Not only did we do this, but this witness and others carried out Roque's idea. Since he was only fourteen or fifteen years old, and the rest of us about the same age, he first discussed it with a religious person. His relatives followed us, and some thirty-six miles outside the city they turned us back from his plan."

Anyone at all familiar with the lives of such saints as Teresa of Avila or Ignatius of Loyola will recall the latter's great ambition to imitate religious heroes, and the charming episode when Teresa, as a child, set out with her tiny brother in quest of martyrdom. In the case of Roque, however, despite the youthful romanticism of the escapade, we note that he first took counsel of a "religious person," making a sort of discernment. Whether the religious person showed good judgment in apparently going along with what was really a very dangerous project, is quite another matter.

Insaurralde continues his testimony, which has so much of the flavor of the epoch that it should be read in full: "Roque progressed in recollection and uprightness of life so much that not only he himself but no one in his presence would utter an oath or obscenity. If they did, he would let them know how he felt. Both in school and in study he was always reckoned the sort of person one would look up to; and he frequently went to Confession and Communion. All his peers admired him."

This testimony, which may seem concocted from stereotypes drawn from lives of the saints, is remarkably reinforced by other classmates of Roque, each with his personal touch. The only slight discrepancy I have found has to do with the escapade into the wilderness. In his own testimony, the Franciscan Luis de Bolaños states that Roque "was about twelve years old" (rather than fourteen or fifteen). He adds a telling detail: "When his relatives found him in the woods and asked why he had left his companions, Roque replied that it was to leave the world and serve God more quietly. But then they all went back to their family house."

Such tiny discrepancies in matters of historical testimony obviously strengthen the broad picture, showing independence of sources rather than untrustworthy collaboration among witnesses.

A final word should be added here regarding Roque's environment. Asunción was at that time not a major colonial capital in any way comparable to Mexico City or Lima, with their viceregal courts and long-established universities. While we possess no precise data regarding the city's population, we are fortunate enough to have a description given by one of Roque's friends,

Ruiz de Montoya, who casually mentions in his *Conquista Espiritual*, that "Asunción has fewer than 400 households, and it is commonly said that there are ten women for each man."

Montoya adds a piquant detail: "There are skilled workmen in all mechanical arts, but nobody considers him an 'expert,' since everyone has learned simply by performing the work in his own house. For example, though the shoemaker makes shoes in public, he does not want to be called a shoemaker, saying that he attained this skill by his own talent. By this metaphysical subtlety he can take care of his own needs and at the same time preserve the nobility inherited from his ancestors, all of whom belonged to the nobility!"

In the Spanish tradition of the day, nobles were supposed to fight and rule, not do manual work. Even the very minor (if indeed real) aristocracy of Paraguay gloried in a profusion of titles; but they preferred, and somehow psychologically needed, servants for what was deemed degrading manual work.

Captured Indians served as a convenience, and this led to the abuses which Roque consistently fought against. The constant unpopularity of the Reductions among the creole colonists was due in large part to this: within the Reduction system, "their" Indians were no longer theirs, but were free citizens under the Spanish crown, no less than any white. Furthermore, Roque and the other missioners never hesitated to dirty their hands working with the Indians; and this, in the colonists' eyes, was a dangerous precedent.

Priesthood

IN DECEMBER 1598, thanks to Governor Hernandarias de Saavedra, Asunción finally enjoyed the visit of a bishop. He was not the recently appointed one, Tomás Vázquez Liaño, chosen January 14, 1596, who died during the long journey to Asunción. He was, rather, Hernandarias's own brother,

Hernando de Trejo y Sanabria, bishop of Córdoba of Tucumán, Argentina.

As already noted, the diocese of Asunción was "widowed" in 1589, following the expulsion of Bishop Alonso de Guerra. The man who was to succeed him, the Franciscan Martín Ignacio de Loyola, would not arrive until 1603. This makes it less surprising that the church of Asunción should take advantage of a renowned visiting prelate to ordain twenty-three young seminarians already prepared to receive holy orders.

Documents suggest that the idea of becoming a priest was suggested to Roque by others. During the beatification process, Father Diego Gordón asserted: "This witness knows that when the said Father Roque González had reached the age when he might be ordained a priest, Bishop Fernando, his father, and other persons of consequence urged him to be ordained. He replied that he felt unworthy, but at the persuasion of the bishop he accepted ordination. In fact, ten years later Bishop Reinaldo de Lizárraga chose him as Provisor and Vicar General of the diocese, but he did not accept this position."

Once again it may seem strange that the exact date of Roque's ordination does not appear in the beatification documents despite their abundance. Hugo Storni suggests the month of December, 1588 as probable, since that period of the liturgical year, Advent, was a normal one for ordinations. On the other hand, José María Blanco believes that the more probable date was March 25 of the following year. He argues from information given by José Guevara, who states that Roque founded Itapúa (Encarnación) on March 25 and named the mission Encarnación "in memory of his ordination to the priesthood."

A coincidence that I find happy, though no other biographer mentions it, is that Roque was ordained by the same bishop, Hernando de Trejo y Sanabria, as was Ruiz de Montoya, the other preeminent founder of Reductions. Montoya, already a Jesuit, was to be ordained thirteen years later, in February, 1611, in Santiago del Estero, Argentina. Like Roque, Ruiz de Montoya was a creole, born in America. Whereas his birthplace was Lima, again like Roque he spent the greater part of his life working for and with the Guaraní Indians of Paraguay.

A remarkable detail in connection with Roque's ordination would seem unthinkable today but was apparently part of the Latin mentality at the time. Father Diego Gordón states: "The day that Roque sang his first Mass in Asunción, his confessors urged him to carry with him during the ceremony the 'palm of virginity' to serve as an example to others. But Roque refused so as not to practice vainglory"! Father Juan Bautista Ferrufino tells the same story, adding a personal note: "It seems that even then, without explicitly intending it, they wanted to foretell that Roque would die a martyr's death." The palm is, of course, used in Chrstian iconography as a symbol of martyrdom no less than of virginity, and the coincidence seemed obvious to Father Ferrufino.

Roque's biographer, José María Blanco, believes that his was the first ordination in the history of Asunción, observing that "this added to the jubilant solemnity of Roque's first Mass." I find it more probable, however, following historian Eladio Velázquez, that Bishop Alonso de Guerra had already performed the first priestly ordinations in Paraguay, including that of Luis de Bolaños and possibly also that of the first Paraguayan secular priest, Rodrigo Ortiz Melgarejo. In any case, Melgarejo, who was to be charged with governing the diocese in 1595, "is chronologically the first native Paraguayan ordained priest."

So it is that, even if Roque's ordination was not the first celebrated in Paraguay, the occasion was one of exceptional interest in Asunción. For apart from Roque, among the twenty-three Paraguayans ordained were Gabriel Riquelme de Guzmán, better known in the Franciscan order as "Gabriel of the Anunciation," as well as a certain Pedro González de Santa Cruz. As we have seen, Roque had a brother named Pedro who was also a priest, but it seems incredible that no document mentions his having been ordained together with Roque. Perhaps there were two priests bearing the same name. In any case, I find the matter puzzling, though of little importance to our subject.

Following his ordination, Roque went to work in the region of Jejuí, then called Mbaracayú, an area containing many Indian tribal groups. True, these indigenous people had been subjected by General Irala within the *encomendero* system from almost the very moment of Paraguay's conquest. Roque, on the other hand, a totally different sort of "conquistador," won over the hearts of the Indians with his combination of zeal and transparent love. The alcade Simón de Mesa declares: "Roque was so beloved and esteemed by the natives of the area, thanks to the example of his life, his teaching, and preaching of the Gospel, that they accepted him thoroughly." Evidently, even as a young priest, Roque was a great missioner.

Crucial to Roque's success with the Indians both here and elsewhere was his mastery of their language, Guaraní, which he had learned from childhood. From the first,

Paraguay had become a biracial and bilingual country. While Roque apparently was entirely of Spanish extraction (though as mentioned, precise documentation regarding his mother is not to be found, which leaves open the possibility of his being Indian), he obviously picked up some Guaraní at least from his playmates. In any case, his eloquence in Guaraní is repeatedly mentioned. Moreover, as Bartomeu Meliá puts it, "Roque did not have to make considerable linguistic adaptations; the creole's adaptation would have to do with subtle dialectical differences; using the same words and living in the same country, he already speaks a different language."

Meliá, who has studied the question more than anyone else and who even wrote his doctoral dissertation at Strasbourg on the topic, goes on: "The missioner is understood, not so much because he speaks the language of the other, but rather because the other's language has become the language of the missioner. Roque did not come from abroad. He lived Guaraní culture during a transformation from within, in a cultural and political process already begun, and of which he is in fact an agent. His adaptation allows him not to be outside the new process." That other great founder, Ruiz de Montoya, was in a different situation, having been born in Lima, in a totally different linguistic area. Montoya learned Guaraní as a missioner, and it is interesting that, thanks to his grammar and dictionary, he, not Roque, is the person deemed the authority on Guaraní. The process mentioned by Meliá had apparently been under way or completed, thanks in great part to Roque, when Montoya came along. (Even today, the authorities most often cited by Paraguayans regarding the Guaraní language, are both modern Spanish-born Jesuits, Antonio Guasch and Bartomeu Meliá.)

Despite his natural eloquence, intensity, and skill in Guaraní, Roque was hardly what one would call an academic person. The superior of the Jesuits in Rome, Muzio Vitelleschi, spoke of him as *"muy gran lengua,"* presumably referring to his mastery of Guaraní; but his provincial superior noted that "when it comes to dealing with Spaniards, Roque is not literary." Obviously, his scholastic training had been altogether informal—in Jerónimo Irala Burgos' words, "not of an academic character"—quite different from standards set in the university centers of Lima or Mexico at that time. Roque was a highly practical man as much by natural temperament as through necessity, and his eloquence was well adapted to the needs of a missioner rather than to those of certain urban parishes, even in a city as small as Asunción was in that century.

As is well known, Jesuits have always focused a great deal of energy on mastering local languages in their mission work. In Brazil and Canada, no less than in China, Japan, and India, they worked hard to become masters of the unfamiliar new tongues. In fact, in China Matteo Ricci was recognized as a master of the Mandarin language, while in Japan the first dictionary of Japanese was published at Nagasaki in 1604 by a team of Japanese and European Jesuits. And four years later the Jesuit João Rodrigues published his *Arte da Lingoa de Iapam*, the first grammar in the entire history of that highly literary people. It is coincidental that at the very time these two books were being published, almost half a world away, Roque, not yet a Jesuit, was working with the natives of Mbaracayú.

The first Jesuit provincial superior of Paraguay, Torres Bollo, was insistent on the importance of "knowing the language, and not in any way whatsoever, but with real mastery." In Paraguay, of course, the Franciscans had already made this linguistic adaptation, and in 1603 the Synod of Asunción had endorsed the directives of the 1583 Council of Lima, making it "obligatory to use the Guaraní language as a necessary means of preaching." Later the Jesuit superior general would ask Roque to teach the language to his companions, since "with this skill much service to the Divine Majesty will be done for the spiritual good of these souls."

We know very little about Roque's specific activities during his years of service in

Jejuí. We know, however, from Simón de Mesa's testimony, that the Indians respected and loved him. More than twenty years later, another witness, García de Céspedes, testified under oath that the Indians "loved him so much that even today his memory is very much alive among them."

It must have been at this time that Roque became even more deeply aware of the injustices of the *encomendero* system. For the region of Mbaracayú produced huge quantities of mate, the tea which is still widely drunk today in Paraguay and in the Southern Cone generally. Its production on a large scale led to exploitation of cheap labor, somewhat like the practice of slavery in the southern United States where cotton dominated the plantation economy. A basic difference, however, was that the Spanish crown explicitly forbade Indian slavery and ordered that the Indians be treated like other persons as "free vassals." Out in the country, far from Asunción, the real treatment of the Indians must have horrified Roque.

In a famous letter addressed to his

49

brother Francisco on December 13, 1614, just a few years after his Mbaracayú experience, Roque vehemently insists on justice for the Indians, "who must be free from the harsh slavery and serfdom of the system; indeed, they are exempt from this by natural law as well as by divine and human law." This important document will be examined later in some detail, and it is reprinted in full in an appendix. In any case, it seems highly likely that during the Mbaracayú years Roque promoted social justice, as far as was possible within the *encomendero* system, as well as working for the specifically spiritual welfare of the Indians. There is no indication of any sudden coonversion on his part before his letter to Francisco.

Some time in 1603 (again we have no way of knowing the exact date), Roque was recalled to Asunción to be rector of the cathedral. The appointment, which probably surprised and distressed him, may have come about because of pressure on the new bishop exerted by the people of Asunción who were eager to have a now famous apostle as their pastor. While this is suggested by other biographers as a likely reason, I find it no less likely that the pressure may have come from *encomenderos* in the Mbaracayú region. Roque was never a man to hold his tongue in the presence of injustice, and his apostolic manner may have been a nuisance to the *encomenderos,* who would have been happy to have him out of the way.

The new bishop was the Franciscan Martín Ignacio de Loyola. On October 9, 1601, he was appointed bishop of Asunción. He was ordained bishop in Valladolid, Spain, and later set out for Buenos Aires, where he arrived on January 1, 1603, along with twenty other Franciscan friars. The bishop's name clearly suggests that he was a relative of St. Ignatius of Loyola, and biographers have always simply referred to him as Ignatius's nephew. More careful research, however, has made it clear that Martín was the grand nephew, not the nephew, of the elder Ignacio de Loyola.

Whether or not the creoles living in Asunción were happy over Roque's appointment to the cathedral, there is evidence that the Spaniards were not. Historian Jerónimo Irala Burgos believes that they were jealous that a creole had been given the post rather than one of their own. The visitor Manrique de Mendoza accused Governor Hernandarias of bypassing Spaniards born in Spain in favor of creoles. Their dissatisfaction, too, at Roque's assignment may have been due to his alleged lack of literary skill (as noted earlier). It is also possible that their accusations to Roque's superior bore some weight. Even so, all other documents indicate that Roque was considered an ideal rector of the cathedral, at least in the eyes of the native-born Paraguayans.

On October 6, 1603, Bishop Martín Ignacio de Loyola called the first Synod of Asunción, and Roque, of course, participated. The synod would require all parish priests and catechists to learn the Guaraní language, "since in it people can be better instructed and will understand Christian teaching better, and they will listen with greater enthusiasm and affection." They were also to teach the catechism of Fray Luis de Bolaños, already referred to.

The synod further endorsed the system known as *reducción de Indios* for the better religious formation of the Indians. The term *reducción* ("reduction" in English) has a very specific meaning in the missionary context. While the Spanish verb *reducir* often means "reduce," as in English, in the mission context its connotation is closer to the original Latin meaning of "lead back." "Gather into settled communities" may be a more accurate paraphrase. In his *Conquista Espiritual*, Ruiz de Montoya explains to his Spanish readers: "We call 'reductions' settlements of Indians who lived in their ancient way in woods, sierras and glens, in hidden arroyos, in three, four, or six houses, now brought together by the work of the Fathers into large towns and into the life of cities and humaneness [and he adds a picturesque detail] to use cotton to dress in, since commonly they used to live naked even without covering what nature intended to be hidden."

As long as the Indians were scattered

far and wide, preaching the Gospel to them was a fruitless task, as early missioners painfully discovered. Furthermore, outside of the Reductions the Indians were always vulnerable to the abuses of the *encomendero* system, which virtually meant slavery. The synod mentioned this danger.

Among other issues, the synod also took up the matter of directing confessors in their counseling work. They were to instruct Christians to respect Indians as free persons; they were to insist on proper salaries for Indians and decent working conditions, as well as respect for their customs; they must make sure that Indians freely enjoy the rights of marriage and family life, as well as the right to return to their own tribes and lands. While we know nothing of Roque's role in the synod, such decisions seem to be very much in line with his thinking and that of Luis de Bolaños.

Bishop Martín Ignacio de Loyola died after a short time in office, on June 9, 1606, while visiting Buenos Aires. His successor, the Dominican Reinaldo de Lizárraga, was already bishop of La Imperial, Chile, when Pope Paul V transferred him to Asunción on July 20, 1609. In a report he sent on September 30 of that year, we are informed that his diocese is "the poorest in all the Indies and has neither gold nor silver," and that priestly personnel is so slight that Asunción itself can hardly be cared for.

MINISTRY

Roque Enters the Jesuits

ASUNCIÓN'S new bishop, Reinaldo de Lizárraga, was evidently so impressed by Roque and his reputation as an exceptional priest that he appointed him Provisor and Vicar General of the diocese.

The bishop must have been taken aback when Roque declined the honor "through humility and holiness," as the documents put it. They go on to add, as if this were some kind of logical consequence, that thereupon Roque entered the Jesuits.

Roque's close friend Gabriel de Insaurralde puts it rather curiously: "As soon as he received the appointment, as though afraid of a court trial to force him to accept it, Roque entered the Order of the Society of Jesus, which he had long wanted to enter."

Six months before he was ordained auxiliary bishop of Villarica, Paraguay, the late

Angel Acha Duarte offered this explanation of Roque's decision: "It is clear that these 'stock phrases' in the biography of the period must not be taken literally as meaning that Christian virtues are not compatible with the service of bishops"! In fact, Bishop Acha Duarte could have mentioned that spiritual books often refer to the episcopal state as one of "perfection." In this case it must seem paradoxical that Roque refused to become a bishop "through humility and holiness."

Roque had known the Jesuits almost from his childhood. In the *Conquista Espiritual*, Ruiz de Montoya devotes several pages to the life of Roque, adding a delightful exaggeration: "Roque grew up in our house—in fact, he thought of it more as his own than he did his father's own house—on the milk of prayer; his perseverance in it made him into a perfect man."

In fact, Roque knew several Jesuits even before he was ordained a diocesan priest. The more appropriate question, then, would seem to be: Why did Roque not become a Jesuit before his ordination? While no certain answer is forthcoming, it seems likely that it was because at that time there was no Jesuit province in Paraguay. In fact, we cannot be sure whether or not he had applied to become a Jesuit before his ordination. When he was actually received into the noviceship on May 9,1609, it was "after many delays," as Marciel de Lorenzana, then rector of the Jesuit community in Asunción, puts it pithily. This may mean that he had been asking to enter for some time past.

In any case, Roque's actual admittance into the Society of Jesus—if not his determination to enter—seems to have been a bit hasty. When the priest Francisco Caballero de Bazán arrived in Asunción with Roque's new appointment, we are informed that "within very few days, abandoning the world, he became a member of the Society of Jesus."

Roque surely knew that a Jesuit normally cannot be made a bishop. In fact, Jesuits who make the "solemn profession" add another vow not to accept ecclesiastical dignities unless "compelled by obedience to someone who can command under pain of sin." These are the very words of St. Ignatius of Loyola.

In Ignatius's Europe, being a bishop implied being a sort of prince. Moreover, a bishop is expected to be "married" to his diocese almost indissolubly, and the bishop's ring is often said to symbolize this. On the other hand, Ignatius expected Jesuits to be fully "disposable," readily movable at a moment's notice, even from one country to another according to the needs of the Church, in a truly missionary spirit. He did, in fact, often transfer his men quite freely. At the same time Ignatius allowed one exception: Jesuits could be bishops in mission lands, where there was real need and no danger of princely wealth or honors. As a result, there are a relatively large number of Jesuit missionary bishops today, especially in very needy areas.

After his own reflections on why Roque became a Jesuit, Bishop Acha concludes: "There is no doubt that such an option and vocation in favor of the poor would be much better carried out by Roque living at the side of those entirely dedicated to the poor: the missionaries, and specifically the Jesuits." This could be more effectively done in the Society of Jesus than in the administrative structure of the diocese of Asunción. Using today's vocabulary, we would say that his personal charism was that of evangelizing the Indians and that his missionary charism was well adapted to the religious order that was being established in Asunción at the time.

Another way of putting it, that can hardly be improved, is that of Irala Burgos: "Roque's desire to dedicate himself thoroughly to the evangelization of the Indians— a task which would be opposed by his fellow creoles and even his own family, who exploited the Indians and justified their exploitation—made his Jesuit vocation altogether logical."

Noviceship

JESUITS have a long-standing custom of keeping in constant touch among themselves and especially with their superior general in Rome. This goes back to Ignatius of Loyola, who insisted on letters being sent to and from Rome with a regularity that must have been extraordinary in the sixteenth century. This wealth of correspondence has made the historian's task at the same time more difficult and easier than it otherwise would have been.

Ignatius was, of course, preoccupied with the problem of unity within an order whose members were scattered all over the newly discovered world. For this, as he wrote, a "very special help will be found in the exchange of letters between the members and the superiors, through which they learn about one another frequently and hear the news and reports which come from the various regions."

Fortunately for historians, anthropologists, and ethnologists, this idea of Ignatius was interpreted in the broadest sense. Ignatius wrote Father Gaspar Berce, one of the first missioners to India, asking for news about everything: "If anything seems exceptional, let us know; for example, unknown plants or animals. Expand the information you send to include general matters, too." (February 24, 1554) It is because of this universal interest that we possess, for instance, the famous *Relations*, written by French Jesuit missioners working in Canada. Between 1632 and 1673 they wrote letters that fill seventy-three large volumes in Reuben Thwaites' English edition. The volumes provide an enormous amount of source material on all aspects of Indian life at the time.

It is also thanks to these "triennial letters," that at last we possess the first precise date known in Roque's life; May 9, 1609, the day he entered the novitiate.

At the same time, we have no document to tell us where his experience as a novice began. Even in 1609 the Society had a novitiate in Córdoba (present-day Argentina) for the new province of Paraguay. But we do have a document dated November 24, 1610, that shows that Roque was then in Asunción. And this leads us to surmise that he was making his novitiate there.

The noviceship, which for Jesuits normally lasts for two years, is a time of deeper spiritual conversion and preparation for years of study and other apostolic work. Roque, obviously, was already something of a veteran. Accordingly, after he had made the Ignatian Spiritual Exercises, a "retreat" lasting some thirty days, he was assigned to a particularly taxing mission in the Chaco, a vast inhospitable tract east of Asunción that is sparsely inhabited even today. He was to work among the unconverted Guaycurús. These nomadic and very warlike people were known to the colonists as more fearsome than any other Indians. In Alvar Núñez's words, "one Guaycurú is the equivalent of twenty Indians from other tribes!"

From a strictly civil viewpoint, the conversion of the Guaycurús and their consequent taming was immensely important, since it would lead to a more peaceful coexistence between the white or mestizo Paraguayans and their neighbors across the Paraguay River in the Chaco. It is understandable, then, that both Governor Hernandarias and the new bishop Reinaldo de Lizárraga (who was to die later that same year) supported the decision of the provincial superior, Diego de Torres Bollo, to send missioners to them. The two Jesuits chosen to go were Vicente Griffi, an Italian, and Roque González, a year younger than his companion.

Torres Bollo wrote an amusing if also tragic anecdote in the *Cartas Anuales* about their experience among the Guaycurús: "It was very comforting to find them now peaceful and 'domesticated' by only two fathers. For this tribe was so barbarous and previously so dangerous to Spaniards—attacking their property and robbing their Indians and children, including even a sister of Governor Hernandarias, carrying off their cattle and horses, burning their crops and making them abandon many lands along the river, waging war for more than sixty years—that their name was reckoned among the Spaniards like that of the very demon himself! Once, in fact, on the night of Holy Thursday, a young boy spotted a toad on the street and cried out 'guaycurú,' which means 'toad' in this country. The shout caused such commotion and terror in the city that some women, not knowing how to escape, drowned in the river, while others tried to hide in church."

The anecdote suggests how demanding the mission was to be. Roque and Vicente Griffi set out across the Paraguay River into the formidable Chaco. With them were only two young altar boys and a Guaraní Indian who knew the Guaycurú language. They did not have a single soldier or sword for their protection. This was to be, quite literally, either a spiritual conquest or a total personal disaster.

Landing in the Chaco, the Jesuits plunged into unknown territory looking for Guaycurú campsites. After a three day search, across rivers and swamps, they finally made contact with several sentinals. It took some persuasion for them to be able to reach the hut of the cacique (or chief), somehow known as "Don Martín Guaycurú." He received them coolly, suspecting some plot, and dispatched spies toward Asunción to watch for any possible movement of Spanish soldiers. Once assured of the missioners' peaceful intentions, Don Martín allowed them to settle in a primitive hovel, which they found uncomfortable even by standards of the day.

Roque and Vicente managed to communicate through their interpreter. In the meantime, they went to work zealously trying to learn the new language, totally unrelated to Guaraní, which was enormously difficult for them. The Indians were naturally suspicious whenever they saw them taking notes, thinking this might be military information for the hated Spaniards. Little by little, however, the cacique began to trust the missioners, even to the extent of going with them to the banks of the Paraguay River near Asunción.

Roque had promised to return to give

his superior some report of their work. Since the cacique brought along with him several Guaycurús to help discover a suitable place to start a mission, the missioners' hopes began to rise.

Unfortunately, two false alarms almost destroyed everything. One was a rumor that the Spaniards had killed one of the Guaycurú leaders. The other, within Asunción, that the Indians had slaughtered the missioners. Roque was able to calm the citizens of Asunción by appearing there in person, and he managed to get help from his brother Francisco, then lieutenant governor, who sent some of his own Indians to persuade the Guaycurús that there had been no murder at all.

The provincial superior received the Indians enthusiastically and later wrote in the *Cartas Anuales;* "After the fathers went there, many Guaycurús came peacefully to Asunción to barter and sell fish and other things. They always come to our house, and despite our poverty we give them as many presents as we can. Their 'domestication' astonishes the Spaniards, especially when they saw the principal cacique come right to the banks of the river, together with many of his Indians, to escort me across and to point out the spot they had chosen for a town and church. I did not want to take anyone with me, except my two companions. Though this seemed very risky to the Spaniards, it did not seem so to me. We were received very enthusiastically, carried on their shoulders through deep swamps where horses could not pass, and after choosing the best site in our judgment and sharing gifts between the cacique and the Indians, I was brought back to the river. The cacique solemnly assured me that he considered it a great honor for me to visit his land, and in gratitude he gave me his word in the name of the Indians to do anything we might ask. He also urged me to hurry back."

At least for the moment everything seemed to be progressing smoothly in the new missionary adventure. Soon, however, the rainy season set in and floods forced the Indians to disperse in search of food. Again the *Cartas Anuales* inform us: "In the five months since I have been back, it has been impossible to do anything among the Guaycurús, partly because Father Griffi has been quite ill and partly because of the river's flooding, which forced the Indians to abandon their lands. When the flood began to subside, Father Roque crossed over and found no trace of the Indians. But he observed that the spot that we had chosen for the reduction had not been flooded. He returned and after ten days two Guaycurús arrived in the city sent by their cacique, Don Martín, to find out how the fathers were faring. Roque returned with them and met the cacique with some two hundred men. They gave him a warm reception and told him that they had not been able to come with their people for the past two months because of the pestilence and the swamps. The father presented them with gifts and came back. This happened in May. Later the Indians returned, and now the fathers come and go very securely."

While Roque was away from his Chaco mission, he dedicated himself to the Indians living in Asunción and established a religious confraternity among them. In a letter to the provincial dated January 19, 1611, he notes: "The custom is still kept of preaching to the Indians in their own language, as well as teaching them Christian doctrine and the ordinary catechism; we also have processions." Processions are, even today, a big part of popular religion in Paraguay and in most parts of Latin America.

Roque would come in from the Guaycurú mission every Saturday, following the provincial's directives. The number of his confraternity members grew steadily, and he wrote that "they celebrate feasts using compositions in their own language, as well as dances, especially the feast of the Circumcision, January 1; all of them praise the Child Jesus in their own tongue and carrying on a conversation with him aloud, lovingly and tenderly; and they thank Him for their redemption and vocation to the Faith."

Meantime, Roque spent weekdays back with his Guaycurús, teaching them how to till the soil, a novel experience for nomads who had not yet entered the neolithic culture. Roque himself would take the lead, regardless of weather, using the plow and instructing by example.

A very interesting letter of Marciel Lorenzana, dated October 19, 1610, reads as follows: "The day before yesterday Roque González went over to the other bank of the river, together with captain Alonso Cabrera, Miguel Méndez, and me. Don Martín received us well and had prepared a fairly good hut for the fathers, in which we lodged. I happened to bring along with me five Indians and two young boys that had come with me from the Paraná. This proved providential. That night we gathered, the cacique and his men on one side, the other Indians on the other, with the children in the middle. I announced: 'I come from the Paraná and bring these children with me. I want these children to teach you the word of God. Listen atten-

tively and let us kneel until I give the signal.'
They obeyed.

The children recited the prayers and catechism and sang their hymns. In the meantime
the Guaycurús listened with great reverence and
attention. Then I told them: 'You know that the
Paraná Indians are very brave and until recently
very warlike, before they heard God's words.
But since God sent me to their land and they
heard his word, they are good and are my good
friends and love me very much. In fact, all their
caciques wanted to come along; but I didn't allow this, since they had to go back to their farms.
I brought only these children to your lands for
you to see what I have told you and understand
that your own children should learn the things
of God like these children. Then they will be
able to teach you.'
They listened with interest and then ap-
plauded. I told them that they should love the
fathers very much, listen to them and trust
them. For the fathers were not seeking their
lands, but only their souls for God, and were
giving them whatever they had. The cacique replied that he loved the fathers very warmly and
trusted them and would listen to them.
I told them, then, that the next day we
would begin cutting wood for the church and

for a cross right where they were meeting. The next day the work began enthusiastically, and my Paraná Indians joined in the activity. The two Spaniards were amazed at their obedience, and I went home quite gratified, since I observed in the Guaycurús a great admiration for the Paranás, now so peaceful, and for their sons who knew Christian teaching so well that the Guaycurú children seemed envious.

Father Lorenzana's enthusiasm for the Guaycurús must have been short-lived, however, since we find no mention in the documents that the church was ever completed. Only much later was a modest chapel built with the lumber. In fact, several circumstances conspired to ruin the mission: hunger following the loss of crops, and the appearance of smallpox, a constant menace to native Americans who enjoyed no immunity against such European diseases.

Even so, many Guaycurús were converted, and during the plagues Roque went on acting as medical doctor, curing the infirm and baptizing the dying. The daughter of a cacique was converted and baptized. Her death brought about the conversion of her father. The Guaycurú custom was for the deceased not to be buried alone; two or three persons had to be killed, in this case little girls. Roque offered to lift the dead child in his arms and carry her to the burial place, while reciting the prayers of the ritual. The cacique felt so honored at Roque's deference that he decided to become a Christian together with his wife and family.

"The Lord willed that while Father Roque was helping them, no single Guaycurú died," wrote Torres Bollo. "We did not stop, night or day, visiting and helping them as well as we could. Since the Indians were very poor, and in March the sickness was at its peak and the cold quite severe, we went out to gather firewood so they could be warm at night. We also gave our blankets to those most in need. At the present time we have baptized some fifty of those who died."

So much for the "active" side of Roque's novitiate. While we know from unanimous testimony that he was a person of intensive prayer, Roque was also known as very dynamic and apostolic as well. The novitiate, as envisioned by St. Ignatius, was not to be geared to the monastic life. Consequently he wanted it to be a testing period with many "trials" or "probations." Ignatius insisted that "in our Society the aspirant must be well tried and long tested at the very beginning. Afterwards, going from one place to the other he has to be in contact with men and women both good and bad. For this kind of life more strength and greater trials are demanded as well as more generous graces and greater gifts of our Creator and Lord." Not many novices in Jesuit history can have had as many such "trials" as did Roque González.

But the novitiate is, in the first place, a time of prayer and the spiritual life. Apart from the core experience—the month-long Spiritual Exercises—Roque kept in close contact with his spiritual director. His provincial superior, Torres Bollo used to propose these simple but intensely practical points for meditation to all the Paraguayan missioners, and obviously in a special way to the neophytes or beginners:

1. Who is sending me? Jesus Christ, who from the cross teaches me how to act. ["Missioner," of course, means one who is sent.]
2. To whom does he send me? To the poorest, most tormented.
3. Who is the one being sent? I, a sinner.
4. Consider how Christ, our Redeemer, worked out our salvation and the redemption of humanity.
5. Consider what Our Lady does for people and how much she loves them.
6. I should see my task as that of the Indians' guardian angel.
7. Consider how St. Paul and St. Francis Xavier did their job, and how I ought to imitate them.

These are hardly astonishing or revolutionary spiritual concepts proposed by Torres Bollo, but they are eminently practical and Ignatian. In the missioner's life, Jesus crucified is the primary model. The missioner is to seek out the most needy, spiritually and otherwise, and try to help them as Christ did. This involves a clear vision of all authentic human values, most of all values that look to eternity. Death is not the final answer.

The role of Mary in this redemptive work is never peripheral in the Catholic and Orthodox tradition. She is the perfectly redeemed model. Ignatius prayed that Mary "place us at her Son's side," and Roque, like other missioners, included her role in his "spiritual conquest." The image he always carried was of Mary at the side of the cross, "La Conquistadora." While we have no authentic copy of this image, it is sometimes thought to be that of Our Lady of Guadalupe, which was already known even as far from Mexico as is Paraguay. It is singularly appropriate in a world of Indians and mestizos. In the modern church of Blessed Roque in Asunción, the image in his hands is clearly that of Our Lady of Guadalupe.

The missioner, while quite aware that he is also a sinner, is that of a surrogate "guardian angel." If modern man may smile at this symbol, or even detect a whiff of paternalism in the image, given the plight of the Indians at the time, it strikes me rather as realistic.

Father Torres Bollo suggests two more earthly exemplars: Paul the Apostle and Francis Xavier, the Apostle of Asia. Although different in their imitation of Christ, they are obviously not proposed as models to be copied. The question is rather: How should one imitate them, in one's own time and space? They are proposed only in view of the apostle's aim "to know Him more clearly, to love Him more dearly, to follow Him more nearly," as Ignatius puts it in the Spiritual Exercises. He does not want just contemplative Jesuits, nor just active, energetic Jesuits, but "contemplatives in action."

Though no document survives to tell us exactly when Roque finished his noviceship and pronounced his vows of perpetual commitment as a Jesuit, we can be reasonably sure that it was two years after the day of his entrance, plus one (according to the Jesuit *Constitutions* and their interpretation). This would mean May 10, 1611.

The simple but moving ceremony would

have corresponded to that used by Jesuits everywhere at the time and nowadays also. It was considered "private" in distinction from the "public" vows pronounced some years later after further experience. The ceremony was probably held in the community chapel of the Jesuit "college" in Asunción, possibly with members of his family present as well. The formula of these vows was composed by St. Ignatius and included in the *Constitutions,* in Latin, the language used by Roque and by other Jesuits until just recently. Its rather stark simplicity, coupled with the courtly language of the time, plus the fact that these words have been used by hundreds of thousands of Roque's confreres, including hundreds of other martyrs, may prove of interest to the reader:

> Almighty and eternal God, I, *N.,* though altogether most unworthy in Your divine sight, yet relying on Your infinite goodness and mercy and moved with a desire of serving You, in the presence of the most holy Virgin Mary and Your whole heavenly court, vow to Your Divine Majesty perpetual poverty, chastity, and obedience in the Society of Jesus; and I promise that I shall

enter that same Society in order to lead my entire life in it, understanding all things according to its Constitutions. Therefore I suppliantly beg Your immense goodness and clemency, through the blood of Jesus Christ, to deign to receive this holocaust in an odor of sweetness; and just as You gave me the grace to desire and offer this, so You will also bestow abundant grace to fulfill it.

The clause "I promise that I shall enter the same Society" constitutes, in fact, a fourth vow and indicates the person's determination to pronounce the other vows in a more public and solemn manner some years later, as directed by superiors. At that later time, Jesuit priests are assigned to be either "solemnly professed" or "spiritual coadjutors." This curious distinction, apparently establishing two classes even among Jesuit priests, not to mention the "coadjutor brothers" (or "temporal coadjutors") must have seemed quite normal in European society at the time, though it has been much criticized since and at times resented in our more egalitarian twentieth century.

Ignatius of Loyola, as early as 1546, secured permission from Pope Paul III to include priests in the Society of Jesus with only very modest theological training, enough for ordinary preaching and administering the sacraments. While these priests were not eligible to hold certain responsibilities in the Society, since their course of preparation had not been as complete as that of others, they were to be fully Jesuits, and the distinction was seldom thought of. Later on, the number of "non-professed" Jesuits increased from six percent at the time of Ignatius's death, to about fifty percent in Roque's day. In recent times, Jesuits have wanted to abandon the distinction altogether, but recent popes have refused the permission, not wanting to change Ignatius's original plan.

Curiously, some ten years after his first vows, Roque was directed to pronounce his final vows as a "spiritual coadjutor." In the same ceremony his friend Pedro Romero (who was also an outstanding missioner, superior of the Reductions, and later also a martyr) pronounced the same vows also as a "spiritual coadjutor." What these two exceptional men had in common was a somewhat abbreviated or informal theological course, as, in fact, did that eminent missioner Antonio Ruiz de Montoya.

By the time of Muzio Vitelleschi, the superior general who approved the last vows of Roque and Pedro Romero, the notion was commonly held that Ignatius only intended men exceptionally skilled in theology—sufficiently so to be seminary professors—to be "solemnly professed." The two young Jesuits later martyred with Roque, Juan del Castillo and Alonso Rodriguez, though already ordained priests, had not yet been admitted to "final vows." In the last analysis, the matter of being "solemnly professed," or "non-professed" or "not yet professed" was of no practical consequence whatsoever.

Few Jesuits in history can have had as strenuous a novitiate as Roque González. In his case we may be sure that the entire novitiate was one long "trial" or "probation," spent largely with the difficult Guaycurús. While there were moments of happiness, as Roque succeeded in converting many of this intractable tribe, he also experienced moments of failure. Such setbacks have inevitably been a central element of missionary experience, from the apparent failure of Jesus and his apostles to the present time. Even as a novice Roque had his share of "job satisfaction" and frustration, learning to accept his own limits and to discover God's providence in all its mystery.

Roque's greatest disappointment, of course, was the failure of his Reduction among the Guaycurús. He was then called to another task, and Pedro Romero took his place; he also met with little success. Finally, in 1626 the Jesuits turned over the Guaycurú mission to the secular clergy, who dropped it after four months, almost a total failure.

True, from the civil point of view the work was not such a loss. The Guaycurús came to live in peace with the people of Asunción. This offered several advantages, including the important possibility of opening a route between Asunción and Chile, both more direct and considerably safer than it had been. But Roque's dream of creating a Christian society—in other words, a Reduction—among the Guaycurú people, never came to pass.

San Ignacio Guazú

ON ARRIVING in San Ignacio, Paraguay today, the visitor sees a fairly tasteless statue dominating the town plaza. Upon asking whom the statue represents, someone will probably reply: "*El Beato.*"When Roque is canonized, the native Misioneros (as the people call themselves, being citizens of the department aptly called "Misiones") may change his title to "*El Santo*," or they may not, as the English still speak of "Venerable Bede," despite his being a Saint and Doctor of the Church.

San Ignacio is called *Guazú* (in Guaraní "big" or "older") to distinguish it from the other San Ignacio Reduction in the Misiones province of Argentina. Actually, both towns are just about contemporary, both having been founded toward the end of 1609 or the beginning of 1610, about the time that Roque was starting his work among the Guaycurús.

The Paraguayan San Ignacio was founded, in fact, thanks to the initiative of a cacique named Arapizandú, whose name appears on a hotel and a new radio station there. Toward the end of 1609, this cacique came to Asunción, in the name of many natives of the area, to ask for priests to instruct them in the Christian faith.

At the time Governor Hernandarias was on his way to Buenos Aires. Arapizandú, therefore, paddled downstream on the Tebicuary and met the governor where that river enters the Paraguay. His request pleased Hernandarias, since up until that time he had faced many problems due to uprisings among the natives. Accordingly, the governor asked Bishop Lizárraga to have some priests sent to serve these people. The bishop refused, either because of a shortage of secular priests or because of a well-founded fear.

The governor then approached the Jesuit provincial, Torres Bollo, and together they went to see the bishop, who still said no. As he put it, he did not want to send any priests to a certain death with no hope of missionary fruitfulness. The provincial then went to the Jesuit college, where he explained both the problems and opportunities, and asked for volunteers.

The rector himself, Marciel de Lorenzana, offered to go, and on December 16 he set out for the remote Paraná area with a Jesuit novice, Francisco de San Martín, and the parish priest of Yaguarón, Hernando de la Cueva, serving as a guide.

After several days the party reached Arapizandú's ranch, on Christmas eve. Nine other caciques offered to help build the Reduction, together with Arapizandú and Father Lorenzana.

But since the location was not quite to Lorenzana's taste, he set out to find the Franciscan missioner, Luis de Bolaños, who was then working near the banks of the Paraná.

Bolaños helped the Jesuits by instructing them in the Guaraní language and giving them sermon outlines in that tongue.

The official founding of San Ignacio occurred in 1610, somewhat farther south than its present site. Then in 1628 it moved to yet another place, perhaps between San Ignacio and Santa Rosa. Only in 1667 was it definitively settled where it is today. This procedure of choosing a tentative site and then moving, even several times, was by no means unusual in Reduction history.

Meanwhile, Lorenzana was called back to Asunción to carry on his duties as rector of the college. Roque González had already joined him to spend some months as an apprentice to the older man.

On May 20, 1612, we are told, Pedro Romero joined Roque and spent a great deal of time trying to learn Guaraní. We are also informed that Roque knew the soul of the Guaraní Indian and felt its needs. In the poetic phrases of Blanco, "wild amid the forests, the Guaranís opened like morning flowers to all the delicacies of culture and learned to moderate their rhythms and to express exteriorly their affections in the theatre and to feel the impetus of piety in all this harmony of sentiment unfolding before the altar; all this in honor of the holiness of their protectors."

This irresistible rhetoric, which would probably make Roque smile, as it does us, describes a reality that was frequently attested to. From the documents it is clear that Roque knew how to make the most of the Guaranís' sensitivity and their zest for music and the other arts. During the 150 years and more of Reduction history, almost all the missioners who wrote of their experiences noted the same traits, although most stressed the Guaranís' talent for imitation rather than their originality.

It need hardly be said that these artistic and musical gifts in the Indians, together with the appreciation of them by the missioners, go far to explain the surprising success of the Reductions during the ensuing

91

century and a half. While René Fülöp-Miller, in *The Power and Secret of the Jesuits*, overstates the case in calling the Reductions "The Musical State of the Jesuits," the sober evidence shows that he had a point.

Even before Roque, of course, other missioners had sensed the charm of music in their apostolic work among the Indians. In Brazil, for example, Manuel da Nóbrega asserted that with enough musician catechists he could convert all of the Indians to Christ. In any case, shortly after Roque's arrival in San Ignacio, the *Cartas Anuales* regularly note the enthusiasm shown by the indigenous people toward music, theatrical events, and sacred dance.

While other Reductions were being developed to the northeast at about this same time, they would soon be forced to move closer to the Paraná area, under the leadership of Ruiz de Montoya, in order to escape from the Brazilian *bandeirantes*. Since the distances these Indians had to traverse were immense, compared to the slight moves of San Ignacio, the latter settlement is commonly cited as the first of the Paraguay Reductions and more or less their prototype.

In a letter addressed to his provincial in 1613, Roque tells something about the daily work routine in San Ignacio. Despite the length of the account, it is well worth reading for the insights it gives into Roque's zeal and his practical administrative sense.

> The countryside near this little town is quite charming, and the climate is excellent, not nearly so apt to cause illness as are some other areas. The fields are fertile, widespread, and large enough to keep some four hundred farmers busy. There is no lack of water and firewood. Nearby forests offer opportunities for hunting, and all sorts of wild animals are plentiful. All this makes it easy for the Indians to forget about fishing, their main occupation in their homeland. The rivers are too far: eight leagues to the Tebicuary and twelve to the Paraná [18 and 24 miles respectively].
>
> Last year there was already something of a harvest. This year there is an abundance, which makes the people very happy. In this town there are some three hundred families, and in the vicinity some four hundred others, enough for another town.
>
> From here the way is open to countless

other Indians, those along the Uruguay River. These have never met a Christian, much less a Spaniard. This makes them more friendly toward us!

I assure you that there will be no better way to reach those people than from here. I have heard this from others who live near the Paraná, who are friendly with them; some are even related to them and are in constant contact with them.

This town had to be built from its very foundations. In order to do away with occasions of sin, I decided to build it in the style of the Spaniards, so that everyone should have his own house, with fixed boundaries and a corresponding yard. This system prevents easy access from one house to another, which used to be the case and which gave occasion for drunken orgies and other evils.

A church and parish house are being erected for our needs. Comfortable and enclosed with an adobe wall, the houses are built with cedar girders—cedar is a very common wood here. We have worked hard to arrange all this; but with even greater zest and energy—in fact with all our strength—we have worked to build temples to Our Lord, not only those made by hands but spiritual temples as well, namely the souls of these Indians.

On Sundays and feast days we preach during Mass, explaining the catechism beforehand with equal concern for boys and girls. The adults are instructed in separate groups of about 150 men and the same number of women. Shortly after lunch, in the early hours of the afternoon, we teach them reading and writing for about two hours.

During catechetical instruction given the boys, all those who are getting ready to be baptized are obliged to be present. Then, after the boys have left, they receive another hour of instruction especially about baptism. There are still many non-Christians in this town; because of the demands of planting and harvesting all cannot be baptized at the same time. Hence, every month we choose those best prepared for baptism; and there are always some left over. Among the 120 or so adults baptized this year there were several elderly witch doctors. [These would be called shamans today.]

During those early years at San Ignacio, Roque was always the sturdy defender of justice and the human rights of the Indians, as well as being pastor of souls and physician of bodies, builder of houses and the church, planter, cultivator and harvester, as well as teacher of agriculture. In the tradition of

Bartolomé de las Casas, Montesinos, and earlier missioners farther north, Roque was horrified by the practices of the *encomendero* system. He, too, was aware of the wide discrepancy between the protective laws emanating from Madrid and the local reality, so far removed from the mother country.

We are particularly fortunate to have a letter written by Roque during his stay at San Ignacio, dated December 13, 1614, addressed to his elder brother Francisco, Lieutenant Governor of Asunción. Since the letter is rather long, rambling, and at times even hard to piece together, I refer the reader to its full text in an appendix. Several of the most relevant paragraphs, however, will be given here; they clearly show how Roque struggled on behalf of the Indians.

The general context of the letter is as follows: The *encomenderos* were furious at the Jesuits, who saw their system as a form of slavery that was contrary to both divine and Spanish law. In fact, the rector of the Jesuit college in Asunción reported that "as a consequence, the people here despise us and tell a thousand false tales against us and refuse to give us alms, even going so far as to refuse to sell us things we need to buy in order to eat."

Since the Indians were beginning to be aware of their rights, "thanks to the defense given them by the Jesuits" (in the words of Jerónimo Irala Burgos), the Lieutenant Governor complained to Roque several times, implying that the Jesuits were causing unrest among the Indians and trouble regarding the labor demanded by the *encomenderos*. The colonists claimed that this labor was in accord with nature. Roque's reply to his elder brother reveals the many conflicts at the time between the Jesuits and the colonists:

> The grace of Our Lord be always with you. I have received your letter and understand from it and from other letters the strong feelings and complaints you have regarding the Indians and especially against us.
>
> In part this was nothing new, nor anything that started yesterday. The *encomendero* gentlemen and soldiers have long complained and even gone further, they have stirred up strong opposition to the Society of Jesus. This, in fact,

does us great honor. I say this because the cause of the Indians is so just and because they have and always have had the right to be free from the harsh slavery and forced labor called "personal service." Indeed, they are exempt from this by natural law, divine and human.

The letter goes on to recount in detail the outrages suffered by the Jesuit community in Asunción and the threats of violence against the Indians of San Ignacio. This became worse after governor Hernandarias set a good example by freeing all the Indians who were serving him. Roque also explains in considerable detail the provisions made by the king, which his brother Francisco did not seem to be aware of at all.

Regarding the *encomenderos* themselves, Roque uses truly prophetic words: "If today a certain number of Indians are rendering this "service," against the King's wishes and those of their caciques, it is because of your threats, even if you do not carry them out and punish them. In order to avoid this harm, some of us are inclined to allow some Indians to go, though others prefer to hold-out for justice, as I myself. Though those that go will suffer now, Our Lord, who sees and knows everything, will provide a remedy. The day is not far away when He will reward services and good deeds and will punish evil ones, especially those committed against the poor.

"The *encomenderos* are in such a state of blindness, that precisely for this reason no God-fearing priest will hear their confessions. For my own part, I tell you that I will not hear the confession of any one of them for anything in this world, since they have done evil and are not willing to admit it, much less are they willing to make restitution and amend their lives. If they do not change and put everything right with the Indians, they will ultimately discover, to their great grief, before Him who is infinitely wise, that they must not cast loaded dice."

What makes this vigorous letter even more impressive is the courage that Roque shows toward his elder brother, Francisco, the head of the González family. Francisco had, in fact, been the family's most influential member, even before his father's death. Moreover, he was sixteen years older than Roque, who shows due deference in the courtly language of the letter. But at the same time, Roque minces no words when he makes his point.

We possess no reply from Francisco to this letter. But there are some hints that even if he was not entirely converted by his brother's sincerity and boldness, at least he was impressed. For the following year he gave Roque written permission to set up three or four new Reductions, "according as he judged best," facing Itapúa. This letter was dated February 23,1615. It was written in the same year that Francisco married one of the sisters of Governor Hernandarias.

At just about the same time that he sent his letter to Francisco, Roque wrote another letter to his provincial, Torres Bollo, on November 26, 1614: "I have been suffering constantly, as I told you when you were here, and even the monthly purges, which you directed, are of no help. I cannot escape and I come close to dying or doing something irrational. *Sicut fuerit voluntas in coelo, sic fiat.* As heaven wills, so be it. Let the will of heaven be done. My will is only to do your will, even if I have to die; since as I have told you on other occasions, my only comfort and delight is to what you want done, since this is the only way I can do what God wants. And although I live here dying and afraid of losing my judgment,—my head is tired out with a continual struggle against many scruples and a sense of loneliness and melancholy—still I assure you that I am determined to remain here, even if I die or lose my judgment many times over. For me this would be no loss, only gain. And so, Father Provincial, you may assign me to any task that you see most suitable for Our Lord's service, since the only thing I want is to be made use of, as you judge best, for God's greater glory."

These poignant lines serve as a corrective to an impression that may have been given in Roque's letter to his brother. These lines show that he is not a man of iron or stone but very much a human being, just as liable to physical and mental suffering as anyone else. Anyone familiar with the lives of great mystics knows that anxieties and scruples like these are by no means rare in their experience. In this letter we see Roque as quite human, far more so that he appears in many of the laudatory descriptions given in the beatification process.

During his years in San Ignacio, Roque somehow found time to complete a project that would continue to be useful long after his death: he translated the third catechism of Lima. The first provincial council of "all the new kingdoms" had been convoked by Jerónimo de Loaisa, archbishop of Lima, in 1551. Its sixth decree states: "We order priests who baptize the natives to question them in their own language, and they should reply in the same." Loaisa later convoked a second provincial council in 1567-68. But the most important of these provincial councils of Lima was the third (according to historian Enrique Dussel), that convoked by St. Toribio de Mongrovejo. This council dealt with the catechism written in Quechua and Aymará, the languages of the former Incan Empire, languages that are spoken even today by Peruvian and Bolivian Indians. This catechism was to become a model for other catechisms and was translated into several native American languages. As we have seen, it had already been translated into Guaraní by Luis de Bolaños, and this translation was approved in 1603 by the Synod of Asunción.

The third catechism of Lima, translated by Roque González, included sermons and prayers expressive of traditional Christian piety. Shortly after Roque's death it was formally approved by another Synod of Asunción in 1631. Experts in Guaraní agree on the absolute mastery which Roque had in that tongue; he had learned it as a child. Little wonder that this work continued to be useful for years and years as an instrument of evangelization.

Toward the end of 1614, after he had prayed the Litany of the Blessed Virgin with his associate Francisco del Valle, Roque felt a strong desire to cross over "the banks of the Paraná in search of the lost sheep of the

Lord's flock." Accordingly, he writes in a letter to the new provincial, Pedro de Oñate: "I left the Reduction and after walking two leagues [*sic*; twelve would be closer to the actual distance] I reached the Paraná and the Lake of Santa Ana. There Our Lord repaid me immediately for the labor of travel—very taxing and through swamps—since I found, among all these pagans, a lone Christian at the point of death. I heard his confession and he died shortly thereafter. I buried him near a cross that we had raised there. I urged the Indians to join in the ceremony. They did so with many signs of love and the desire of salvation."

New Reductions

AT THIS POINT in his life, Roque was working near the Paraná, one of the world's most majestic rivers. "I went upstream," he writes. "Near an Indian village I heard the sounds of crying. I asked what was the matter and was told that a young child had just died. Hurrying to him, I found him still breathing. I baptized him, and thereupon he died. The strange workings of divine Providence! On their way back to the village the Indians told me that they were rowing simply to race, for no other reason than for fun. But the Lord had chosen that particular Indian and would save him and have him baptized while they were racing."

Roque walked into various Indian settlements apparently without any fear whatsoever. His intention, as he put it, was "to give them the chance to know their God and Creator, to adore and reverence Him." A surprised cacique asked: "How have you dared to come here where no Spaniard has ever set foot? Don't you know that I made this land and this sea, and that everybody here obeys me?"

Roque replied fearlessly: "No you didn't. God is the cause of everything." The cacique then began to ask more questions about God and other religious matters. He also began to show some affection for Roque.

At the same time, however, he told him to turn back.

Again Roque answered: "No, I didn't come here in order to turn back; I came to teach you and your people the path to heaven." The place where they were talking seemed appropriate for a Reduction, and Roque said so, adding that he wanted to erect a cross there. In a letter he adds: "and they themselves, though pagans, helped me to raise the cross."

At about this time Roque had to interrupt his missionary travels and go back to Asunción for more men. He also needed permission to found new Reductions and he needed to define precisely the jurisdictional boundaries of his future apostolate. He wanted to avoid all possible ambiguities and conflicts regarding the missions. Accordingly, we have a document dated February 23, 1615, signed by Roque's brother Francisco which reads as follows: The fathers of the Society of Jesus, with much charity and zeal for God Our Lord and for his majesty the King, have persuaded many pagan Indians to settle peacefully in Reductions in convenient places where they can be taught our holy Catholic faith; for this reason and for other motives, in the name of his Majesty and in virtue of the powers I possess, I hereby grant license and permission to Father Roque González de Santa Cruz, of the same Society, or to any others of the same Society of Jesus, to set up, in his Majesty's name, three or four Reductions in places that seem best, and in particular in places facing Itapúa on the opposite bank of the Paraná and on the Lake of Santa Ana. And I order, under penalty of a fine of 200 pesos, that no one of any state or condition whatsoever, in any way dare to obstruct or impede the said Reductions. If anyone does impede or causes them to be impeded, he will be rigorously punished by the said penalty as one attempting to hinder something so holy and of such service to God Our Lord and to his Majesty."

This document was composed by his brother scarcely ten weeks after Roque's vigorous letter to him, and it suggests either a conversion on the part of Francisco, or perhaps simply a sense of relief. If Roque were to start new Reductions far from Asunción, there would be less trouble for Francisco in the capital, where many *encomenderos* lived. The farther the better! Whatever Francisco's motivation, Roque now had a green light for wider apostolic ventures.

When Roque returned to the place where he had set up the cross, he was delighted to see the Indians there zealously defending it, "as though they were already Christians of longstanding. For when other caciques and Indians from upstream wanted to tear the cross down, the local Indians took up arms to defend it."

Roque then waited two months for the arrival of a brother Jesuit, Diego de Boroa (1585-1657). Boroa arrived on Pentecost Monday and took up residence with Roque in the small hut which also served as the chapel.

Though a native of Paraguay, Roque felt all the discomforts of a missionary. He wrote: "We need just about everything. The cold, against which there is no defense, was such

108

that we could not sleep. As for food, we sometimes eat a bit of cooked maize, at other times flour of mandioca which the Indians eat. And since we used to send to the field for certain herbs that parrots eat, the Indians whimsically called us parrots!" Mandioca, or manioc, something like an unsweet yam, is a staple of Paraguayans and neighboring peoples even today. I find it strange that Roque should complain about it, since it is the staple of poor people here. Obviously the Spaniards had not yet taken to it. The cold, which he also mentions, is always an unpleasant surprise to newcomers, save for the affluent who live in well-built heated buildings. The rest of us dread winter more than summer, here in this semitropical region.

It was only natural for some Indians to suspect that Roque and Diego were "spies and false priests, and that through our books we were bringing them death." Still, as Roque wrote, "little by little they are seeing the light and recognizing that we are genuine fathers to them, giving them with a father's love whatever they ask for. And we are their doctors as well, not only of their spirits but also of their bodies, helping them day and night when they are ill. We worked to build a little church, tiny and thatched; and the poor Indians marvelled at it as though it were a royal palace. We also took turns doing rough plaster work to show them how to do it, since previously they didn't even know mud-daubing. Everything was finished for the feast day of our holy father Ignatius, July 31, 1615.

Five years later, in the 1620 *Cartas Anuales*, another writer describes the beauty of the Itapúa: "It is in such a lovely, charming spot that even a painter's brush could do no better save for the luxuriance of meadows and groves. About a league and a half away there is a cove that seems like a sea. From our lodgings we can see through its narrow mouth all the canoes coming from upstream, from the Igañá and Yguazú and on to the Uruguay, which is nearby. And since the fathers have their hearts entirely set on winning over the three provinces that can be seen here, one can hardly imagine anything more delightful or recreational."

Roque's picture of the place, five years earlier, was more matter-of-fact: "We placed a bell in the wooden belfry. This had never been seen before in the country and naturally caused amazement. What gave us great satisfaction was the fact that the Indians themselves raised a cross in front of the church. After we explained why we Christians venerate the cross, together with them we went down on our knees. Though this is the last one set up in this area, I trust in the Lord that it marks a beginning for many others to come." As we know, it was to be anything but the last.

In the same letter Roque, almost parenthetically, includes details that interest us. It was the feast of Ignatius Loyola, 1615, (not to be canonized until 1622), and Roque and his companion Diego de Boroa took advantage of the occasion to renew their vows. While the vows which Jesuits take after their novitiate are meant for life, there has always been the custom of "renewing" them frequently in private and twice a year in the presence of others. In fact, four years later, Roque and Diego, together with Pedro Romero, were to pronounce their final vows in this same church.

Roque mentions, too, that they tried to celebrate the feast day with all sorts of "merrymaking, considering the few possibilities available. We tried to include dancing, but the boys are still so rough and rustic that the project failed." Later, of course, in the history of the Reductions, religious dances were to become quite popular and successful, as we know from many eyewitness accounts. At this point in their development, however, the tradition had not yet taken hold.

Two days before the feast of Ignatius, the fathers were delighted by the arrival of a "cacique from the Uruguay region who came to see us and was so pleased and enthusiastic that he would come back to our Reduction after harvesting." Roque seemed almost obsessed by the Uruguay region and its missionary possibilities.

"A little later," he adds, "I went down to the Lake of Santa Ana." He spent three months arranging for this Reduction. But despite his authorization to found it, he seems to have entrusted it to the Franciscans, since it is never mentioned again in the Jesuit documents.

When Roque returned from Santa Ana at the beginning of November, he was informed that the governor was six leagues downstream and that he wanted to visit them. Roque writes: "I sent down a party of ten canoes and their caciques to meet him. They invited him to visit their city."

Roque continues the account: "The Governor arrived with forty soldiers. Before disembarking he went very piously to reverence a cross that we had just raised in the middle of the great Paraná River [possibly on the island at the new bridge spanning the giant river between Posadas and Encarnación]. We received him with much affection and gave him as much hospitality as our poor resources allowed. He appeared quite grateful and delighted with the Reduction, which is already large, well situated, and with streets. He said he was amazed that so much could have been done in three years [*sic*]." He added that he was particularly surprised to find the Indians attending Mass so peacefully "where no Spaniard had previously set foot, and he couldn't get over the way these Indians had abandoned their lands, relatives, and property to come and settle there with the father."

But life in Itapúa was no earthly paradise. Toward the beginning of the following year, 1616, Brother Boroa was transferred to San Ignacio and replaced by Francisco del Valle. Roque wrote of new sufferings: the crops were lost and the people were in deep misery. "Their poverty extends to real necessities. They started Lent eating a single egg and continued on eating wild thistles until Our Lord provided some vegetables thanks to a Franciscan who knew how much they were suffering."

That Franciscan was, unsurprisingly, Luis de Bolaños, who was always a good friend and support. Bolaños told the story later on while he was giving testimony for Roque's beatification: "Knowing what was

114

going on, this witness sent Father Roque many Indians from the Reduction of Yutí, loaded with flour from mandioca roots, to give him and his Indians something to eat."

Another trial, as we read in the 1618 *Cartas Anuales*, came from the threat of war: "The colonists sent a company of soldiers from Asunción to punish certain rebellious Indians. This started the rumor along the river that they were coming to attack everybody. The river boiled with canoes crossing from one side to the other, all in confusion and panic. Only those Indians in our Reduction felt any security, since they were under the protection of the Fathers."

Roque hurriedly wrote to the Spaniards that it was "very important for them to turn back. And to reassure the Indians, he went personally, after sending the letter, to negotiate the dispute. He did this after sending away all the Indians of the Igañá quite satisfied. When Roque arrived, the Spaniards had already received his letter and had turned back."

The third trial was a "pestilence of catarrh and fever which struck down almost everybody. Even Father Francisco del Valle fell a victim, leaving only Roque to do the work in Itapúa and Yaguapoá." Somehow Roque was strong enough to carry on, day and night, hardly resting at all, "caring for their temporal and spiritual welfare."

The year 1616 had started with the foundation of Yaguapoá. By the end of 1618 or the beginning of 1619, the provincial, Pedro de Oñate, paid a formal visit there, officially inaugurating the new Reduction.

One surprising fact should be added to this chapter: it is our uncertainty about the actual location of this new Reduction. Several ancient maps place Itapúa on the left bank of the Paraná, where present-day Posadas stands (capital of the Misiones province of Argentina); while Yaguapoá is shown on the right bank, a bit downstream. On the other hand, other maps place Itapúa where Encarnación stands today. José María Blanco inclines toward the Posadas location. His grounds are references given by Roque to Itapúa as the "gateway to the Uruguay," which seems to suggest that to go from Itapúa to the Uruguay river one would have to cross the wide Paraná.

Toward the Uruguay
(1619-1625)

WRITING from Córdoba, Argentina on February 17, 1620, Father Pedro de Oñate describes the site of Roque's next undertaking. "The Uruguay is an immense river, almost as large as the Paraná. It is approximately half a league wide [a mile and a half] and runs parallel to the Paraná, not far from our residence of Itapúa, before flowing down to the sea. Almost 300 leagues downstream it enters the giant Paraná slightly above Buenos Aires. No one knows its sources, though it is said that they are in the hill country of Brazil. On its banks, between Itapúa and the spot where it enters the Paraná, a considerable number of Indian settlements are known to exist. Those best acquainted with

117

the area put the number of Indians at more than sixty thousand and call them naturally good and peaceful."

From Itapúa to the first Uruguay villages "there are only some eighteen or twenty leagues. So it is that they are often talked about and that Father Roque González, a famous linguist and fervent, experienced worker, several times entered the nearest villages and found there a friendly attitude, even a desire of the people to become Christians. He also received a great deal of information about the countless throngs of people downstream."

Oñate goes on to say: "When I went to these Reductions, I saw the abundant harvest that the Lord has ready for us there and is already disposed to gather into His granaries. And since our province now has a number of members, and moved by the insistence of our men here in the Paraná area in favor of this, I left two fathers in each of our three residences and decided that Roque González should start this new vineyard of the Lord with the plow of the Gospel."

Oñate provides several more details on Roque's preparations for his new adventure. Several Indians had come to see Roque, among them a leading cacique. Diego de Boroa brought the Indians to the church, where they were much impressed by the ornaments and images, especially by the painting of "the Four Last Things done by Brother Luis." This "Brother Luis" was the Frenchman Louis Berger, born in Abbeville in 1589. In 1614 he became a Jesuit as a "coadjutor brother," having already been trained in painting, music, and dancing. He arrived in Buenos Aires in 1617 and worked in the missions until his death in 1639, making full use of his versatile artistic talents. The documents often mention how much Louis Berger was appreciated by his fellow missioners.

Before setting out, Roque made the Spiritual Exercises once again and pronounced his final vows as a Jesuit together with Pedro Romero on October 20, 1619. As we mentioned before, the future martyrs were not invited to the solemn profession but to the status of spiritual coadjutors in the

Society. Curiously, as it seems to us, Diego de Boroa was solemnly professed in the same place only two days earlier. He would later become provincial of all the Paraguayan province, from 1634 to 1640, while his more famous confrere was to be given the lesser responsibility of "superior of the Guaraní missions."

Boroa describes the vow ceremony of his two friends as "an immense consolation for me, as well as something of a humiliation, as I saw these two giants of Christian virtue right before my eyes. They took their vows with the greatest celebration that we could afford, in the presence of a huge gathering of Indians from several nearby Reductions." Boroa seems almost embarrassed at the thought of men that he looked up to, now somewhat less evaluated by the order than he himself was. This is not an exceptional experience among Jesuits even today.

The next day Pedro Romero returned to his post, while "Roque worked enthusiastically on preparations for his departure, which took place yesterday, the 25th, the feast of the holy martyrs Chrysanthus and Daría [a Roman couple buried alive on that day in the year 183]. In the morning, with the altar and church bedecked as on a major feast day, we rang the bells and explained to the people why they had been summoned for Mass. We asked them to pray for the conversion to the faith of the people of the Uruguay region in response to the word of God that would be preached to them by Father Roque. Embracing him warmly, we assured him of the happy outcome of his new mission which was begun with such clear signs of Our Lord's will."

Later chroniclers told of the problems Roque had to face and especially of his "encounter with an armed multitude that tried to cut off his way." Even so, evidence of his contemporaries and a letter from Roque himself describe "caciques coming to welcome him and expressing joy at his arrival." On December 24, 1619, Boroa wrote about the "good news of caciques from the Uruguay region going out joyfully to speak with Roque. I received a letter from him yesterday in which he mentions that he discovered a fine spot for the Reduction that you were so concerned about. It has a fine, handsome forest a short league from the Uruguay, and the caciques there are happy over the prospect of having both a chapel and a church bell."

Boroa sent carpenters to help in the construction. They arrived in November, and in two weeks they had the new cross, a small church, and the belfry all built. Since this was the feast of the Immaculate Conception, the Reduction was named "Concepción."

Unfortunately for Roque's biographers, the *Cartas Anuales* break off at this point and are not continued again until 1626. These were among the many documents that were scattered at the time of the Jesuits' suppression in 1773.

This gap leaves us uninformed about an event that meant a great deal to the missioners in Paraguay and elsewhere: the celebration of the canonization of Ignatius Loyola and Francis Xavier in 1622. A later Jesuit missioner and historian, Nicolas du Toit (a Frenchman born in Lille on November 28, 1611, who would pronounce his last vows in Encarnación in 1649), tells us something of Roque's participation, according to sources available to him:

> The spectacle that stirred most interest and seemed most novel was provided by some children in Asunción. Father Roque González directed them and had them divided into two groups, one Christian and the other pagan, who acted out a battle. While the idolators were bedecked with colorful plumage and armed with bows and clubs, the Christians' only weapon was the cross. All moved in ballet style to the rhythm of music. It was something to see—their feigned attacks and defense, all in dance step. After a while, the musical battle was over, and the Christians carried off the conquered pagans to judgment. Thereupon the prisoners fell to the ground, but then lept joyfully in their voluntary captivity and suddenly ran to the altar of Saints Ignatius and Francis, thanking them because their sons had introduced Christianity to Paraguay. Father Roque González had brought along with him the famous cacique Guarecipú and twenty-three Uruguayan catechumens [new

123

converts preparing for baptism]. They were then all baptized amid the public joy of the whole college, and Governor Manuel Frías served as their godfather.

Unfortunately we have neither a letter nor a message from Roque himself describing this visit to his home city of Asunción. It would be interesting to know whether he felt any scruples at this sort of display (which some people today would call "triumphalism") or whether he was a man of his time with a taste for such spectacles as he was in so many other ways. In either case, he surely must have been happy to bring to Asunción the first fruits of these apostolic efforts. One historian speaks of this event as "an oasis amid the bitter moments" of Roque's mission work.

The provincial of Paraguay who succeeded Pedro de Oñate, Nicolás Mastrilli Durán (a Neapolitan who was later to serve also as provincial of Peru), had this to say: "All of us found these Indians inaccessible, since they resisted any contact with the Spaniards, who never dared enter their territory. Only Father Roque González had the courage to plant the standard of our salvation where the standard of Spain had never been raised. He did this by founding the Reduction of Concepción, as reported in the last *Cartas Anuales* [mentioned above as lost]. But for the past three years this new Reduction has suffered terribly from the plague. Only some sixty families have survived. While the plague lasted, all one could hear, day or night, were the moans of the sufferers. Roque was tempted to give up the project altogether, seeing such slight results, and to go on to another one more in line with his apostolic eagerness, in nations not yet converted."

The same provincial visited Roque in Concepción. "I encouraged him to set out downstream and discover the lay of the land. He did so, and at considerable risk he walked several leagues, until he spotted behind him a group of Indians ready to kill him. He escaped thanks to a marvelous ruse that threw them off his track." He kept to his path, moving swiftly with the Indians in pursuit, until nightfall. Then he built a large campfire on the bank of the river where they expected him to spend the night. But when the Indians crept up to the campfire, Roque had long since made his escape. Obviously this practical sense was no small part of his apostolic equipment.

San Nicolás, San Francisco Javier, and Yapeyú

AFTER finally getting the Reduction of Concepción fully on its feet, Roque felt free to open up other parts of the vast Uruguay region. Much like the more celebrated Jesuit missioner, Francis Xavier, Roque constantly felt inspired to push on.

On the Piratiní River, a tributary of the Uruguay, Roque came upon a spot that seemed ideal for a new Reduction. The date was May 3, 1626, the feast of the Finding of the Holy Cross, when he celebrated his first

Mass in that area. In tribute to his provincial, Nicolás Mastrilli Durán, he called the new foundation "San Nicolás." In the *Cartas Anuales* the provincial sketches something about this event, without, of course, suggesting the origin of the Reduction's name:

Reduction of San Nicolás of the Piratiní. This is the second Reduction founded by Father Roque González in the Uruguay region. It is seven leagues from Concepción and is situated on the River Piratiní, which empties into the Uruguay.

A large number of people joined this Reduction, so large, in fact, that a terrible famine ensued. Father Roque stated that he had never experienced a worse one. Even so, within two months 280 families joined, and within a few more months, 300 others. Today the number is somewhere around 500 families.

The land here is quite fertile and is suitable for a large population. We have good reason to hope for this before long. The leading cacique, who first received Father Roque, has shown good signs of constancy in his sufferings and in the diligence that he has shown in founding the town.

Mastrilli Durán's first visit to the new Reduction bearing his name was an occasion for jubilation. His narrative goes on: "The Indians were so joyful that they had me spend the night outside of town, so exuberant was their celebration with songs and instruments. In the morning they all came out to receive me, rushing to kiss my hands. I was afraid I would be smothered in the bustle had the two fathers with me not moderated their enthusiasm."

By a decree of December 16, 1617, the former civil province of Río de la Plata was divided in two. Asunción was made the capital of the region called Guairá, including the cities of Villarica del Espíritu Santo and Santiago de Xérez. Buenos Aires was made the capital of the other, called Río de la Plata, which included the cities of Santa Fe, San Juan de Vera de las Siete Corrientes, and Concepción del Bermejo (roughly present-day Paraguay and Argentina). The ecclesiastical division into two dioceses followed and was approved by Rome on March 16, 1620.

In September of 1623 Don Francisco de Céspedes was appointed governor of Río de la Plata. Wishing to push ahead with the *conquista* and knowing that Roque was at the moment in a Reduction on the Uruguay, he tried to get in contact with him. Hernando de Zayas brought letters from the governor to Concepción. Again we are informed by Mastrilli Durán's *Cartas Anuales*:

> It is hard to express the happiness of all the fathers in the Paraná Reductions, and especially that of Father Roque González, when he realized that God was inviting him to go where he had not dreamed possible, through the open door that he had not previously been able to break open with many labors.

Given the importance of this new opportunity, Roque decided to travel to Buenos Aires in response to the governor's invitation. Durán adds some interesting details:

> During his journey Roque met a large flotilla of canoes heavily loaded with more than 400 Indians geared for battle. In great rage they were on their way to attack another nation which they felt had offended them. Roque was not in the least upset at finding himself in the midst of such warlike people who had never seen the face of a Spaniard before. He proceeded to speak to them with great energy and courage, asking

them to turn back from their purpose. Sensing his great eloquence and charm, they listened very attentively—all the more so when they discovered that the speaker was Father Roque González. While they had never seen him, they had heard a great deal about him, for his reputation had even reached their lands.

When Roque finished his speech, the Indians said how happy they were to hear his moving words, which were even more powerful than his reputation had led them to expect. In fact, they had been eager to meet and hear him. To please him they abandoned their project, inspite of their strong desire for revenge.

Roque reached Buenos Aires together with several Indians from his Reduction on the feast of St. John the Baptist—which must be the feast of the saint's birth, June 24, not that of his death, July 4.

The governor gave the following authorization: "Inasmuch as I have given over to the Society of Jesus, in the name of his Majesty and my own, the provinces of the Uruguay for the settlement of the natives and their conversion to the holy Catholic faith, and the obedience and service of his royal Majesty; and since this is to be brought about by means of reductions or towns that the fathers of the same Society are to establish among the same natives; in the name of his Majesty I give full authorization and power, with no limitation or restriction, for them to found all the reductions as they see fit in the name of his Majesty and my own, giving them both authority and symbols of authority, as far as they judge suitable for the service of both Majesties." This document, preserved in the Biblioteca Nacional of Rio de Janeiro, is of major importance, as is another one in which the governor specifically mentions Roque, "who has come in person to pay me obedience."

The governor asked the rector of the Jesuit college in Buenos Aires, Juan Bautista Ferrufino (a Milanese Jesuit who would later be provincial of both the Chilean and Paraguayan provinces) to send along with Roque the Peruvian father Miguel de Ampuero. Ferrufino approved, and Ampuero set out with Roque. On January 28, 1582, Ampuero made his solemn profession in the Reduction of San Nicolás.

Back in his Uruguay missions, Roque went to work vigorously to establish the new reductions. Yapeyú was planned and started, though not finished until February of 1627. In the meantime, Roque tried to consolidate San Francisco Javier.

But the new governor made a serious mistake that almost ruined the entire undertaking. Mastrilli Durán writes that he sent a Spaniard "and two others of the land with title of *regidores* to take part in our Reduction of Concepción and the surrounding region. The misconduct of these *regidores* so enraged the Indians, who had been suspicious of them from the start, that it took all the authority of Father Roque and of the provincial to prevent them from tearing the *regidores* to pieces. When the governor was informed, he ordered them back."

This imprudence of the governor was nearly disastrous, for the cacique of Concepción had recognized the authority of the

Spanish crown on the condition that it would never actually subject the Indians to the immediate rule of the Spaniards, but only to the fatherly care of the missioners. We know, in fact, that for some time after this happened, San Javier "had fewer people than the other Reductions—no more than 300 souls—since so many people fled back to the woods when the Spaniard threatened to hang an Indian if he refused to join the Reduction with his people."

After the Spaniards departed, things went along more peacefully. Mastrilli Durán writes: "When the scandal was over, the country became calm again. The Indians remained well disposed to establish a great Christian society. This is now being done for God's glory and in spite of the hell [sic] raised by this stormy situation. In fact, in a short time four more Reductions have been founded, apart from Concepción."

This episode shows the natural tension that existed between the civil authorities and the spiritual concerns of the missioners. The

Jesuits' vision was clear and quite different from that of the colonizers: for the missioners a reduction was meant to be a haven of salvation. The Uruguayan historian Juan Villegas puts it well: "For the Jesuits generally and for Roque González in particular, the project of the reductions meant a series of activities whose purpose was the evangelization and salvation of the Indians." And Roque himself added in his strong letter to his brother Francisco, "a place where the Indians would be free from every sort of slavery, as free men directly under the Spanish crown."

The Yapeyú foundation was to enjoy a remarkable future, eventually becoming one of the most important Guaraní reductions. As he describes it, Mastrilli Durán personally participated in this establishment:

> This is the fourth Uruguay reduction, not in geographical order, but in order of founding. It is on the banks of the Uruguay river, just above one of its tributaries called Yapeyú, thirty leagues downstream from Concepción and a hundred from the port of Buenos Aires. It is the

closest of all the settlements to that city.

When I went to Guayrá, I left Father Roque with instructions to go down to this land and establish a Reduction. He did so. Since few people were to be found there at the time, and we had a shortage of priests, the number of Indians did not seem sufficient to warrant a foundation that would occupy Jesuits who were needed elsewhere. When I returned from Guayrá, I was more and more convinced that we should occupy this place, and I determined to go there personally with Fathers Roque and Pedro Romero, to begin the Reduction with whatever Indians were there, however few they might be.

We made the journey and found only three long huts there with a hundred Indians. They received us joyfully. We distributed some things we had brought to win over their good will. They were quite friendly and delighted that we wanted to found a Reduction there. They happily started to work on February 4, 1627, and before I left they had cut down enough wood to build a fine church on the spot I had designated. They also began work preparing the soil for sowing crops, *which is the first thing done when founding each of our Reductions* [emphasis in the original]. Preparing the soil is essential because the Indians do not sow in an open field and the soil, being exhausted, is not very productive.

I brought the Yapeyú Indians a quantity of metal wedges to help them construct their town.

By the end of the same February they had already built both church and rectory. So it was that Father Pedro Romero began his fruitful work as pastor at Yapeyú. *I left him there alone.*

The words cited in italics above reveal Roque's strong practical awareness and that of the other mission founders. If the Reductions were to serve as quasi-utopias, privileged havens of peace and security for evangelization, they needed, first of all, a secure supply of food. Even so, we know that the first steps in several reductions were difficult even on this score, both for Roque and for the others. They had to win over the confidence of the Indians before their sowing of plants or the Gospel could show any results.

Yapeyú, or to use its full name, Yapeyú de los Reyes, would later become the great musical center of the Reductions. After Roque's time, among the various missioner-musicians who created this school at Yapeyú for the best native musicians the best known is Antonio Sepp (1655-1733). Sepp was a Tyrolese who had been trained in Vienna, London, and other musical capitals before becoming a Jesuit. He was surely one of the most exceptional factotums in Reduction history.

Sepp was not only a performing musician but also a craftsman of musical instruments, and a skilled teacher of a dozen or so different instruments. In the single year of 1692, as he reports, he "trained the following future music masters: six trumpeters, four organists, eighteen cornetists, ten bassoonists, [and more than thirty masters of baroque instruments which are no longer used today]. All this gives incredible satisfaction not only to the missioners here, who show their gratitude by giving me tidbits from time to time (such as honey, sugar, and fruit), but especially to the Indians. They are very happy and treat me so well that I blush to mention it, since I turn all to the glory of Our God and Lord!" It was Sepp, too, who introduced the pipe organ with pedals to South America, and tradition maintains that he also introduced the harp, Paraguay's national instrument.

Like other missioners, Sepp was

impressed by the natural musical talent of the Guaranís: "The characteristic of their genius, is in general, music. There is no instrument whatsoever that they cannot learn to play in a short time. And they do it with the skill and delicacy that one admires in the most gifted masters.

It is in great part thanks to the musical school at Yapeyú that music because so famous in the Reduction tradition. Yet the origins of Yapeyú, as of other Reductions, are credited to the pioneer work of Roque González, Pedro Romero, and other missioners of the first generation.

From Ibicuití to Carró

TOWARD the end of February, 1627, the provincial, Mastrilli Durán, appointed Roque to be superior of all the Reductions in the Uruguay area and authorized him to found yet another mission there.

138

The banks of the Ibicuití River were reported to have a large number of inhabitants, and this led Roque to start upstream in another quest. After traveling about fifty leagues, he finally contacted a people belonging to the Tabacán tribe.

Though once again Roque was the first white man ever to meet these Indians, as soon as he began speaking, he was well received, thanks both to his eloquence and to the gifts he had brought along with him. They carved a wooden cross to place upright, and they demonstrated such enthusiasm that "old men, children, and even women" helped celebrate the founding of this new town. Roque celebrated Mass in a small improvised chapel, naming the new Reduction Candelaria (Candlemas), for the principal liturgical feast in the month of February.

After a while Roque had to leave Candelaria in order to carry out his new obligations as superior of the other missions as well. He promised to be back soon, bringing whatever was needed to advance the

Reduction. He also promised to stay with the people upon his return until he could send another priest to take his place.

Roque, however, was never able to carry out his promise, since other Indians of the Tapé region attacked the new mission and dispersed its inhabitants. When the bad news reached Roque, he went back, gathered the people again, and persuaded them to accompany him to a high sierra and build a better Reduction there.

In his account Roque states: "I walked freely among them, though with deep pain, because in all the Tapé area there is no place to settle 200 families together. Formerly these Indians were a numerous people; now they live in tiny villages, the largest containing a hundred Indians."

Roque goes on: "At last, I determined to go back, though a bit puzzled, because God allowed the Indians on the other side of the range to get together to attack and rob me. As I got under way, we heard rumors of this. The people who had brought me here went out to meet them, but the hostile

Indians threated to throw me out again. At this my people returned, frightened at the thousand threats hurled at them. So I decided to go back, seeing evidently that this was Our Lord's will.

"Having done all I could and having risked my life twice so as not to leave those poor souls unprotected, I saw everything I wanted to do being undone and all hell up in arms against me. I can truly say that of all my humble labors and voyages none have been so dangerous as those in Ibicuití and Tapé.

"But all this is nothing compared to what we owe to the Lord for whom it is done. And if the purpose of this is to disenchant us from the fascination of Ibicuití and all Tapé, I would consider all the trouble worthwhile, since it was all done under holy obedience. On the way back I had a chance to scrutinize the land and observe how the Indians of Ibicuití lived. So now I can give an accurate report on this whole region."

Roque's letter goes on to describe territory that was still unknown to the Spaniards:

"It is at least 300 leagues long and in some places more than 100 leagues wide [roughly 900 by 300 miles]. All these lands are inhabited by Indians, but they are very scattered. The entire area must include about 20,000 people. Between the rivers there is an important stream called Aix, where according to the Indians the Portuguese used to enter in small boats, leaving their ships on the high sea. They came to barter with the Indians, bringing clothing much like my own and hats."

Roque went back to San Nicolás to head inland. This led to the foundation of another Reduction, to which he gave the same name as the one that had failed, Candelaria.

The man who succeeded Mastrilli Durán as provincial, Francisco Vázquez Trujillo (1571-1652), describes these events: "Roque returned to the Reduction of Los Reyes [Yapeyú], and from there set out upstream on the Uruguay until he reached Concepción, two leagues from the Uruguay in the direction of the Paraná. There he learned from the Indians that it would be easy to enter the

142

Ibicuití, Tapé, and Mbiaza by way of the Reduction of San Nicolás del Piratiní, five leagues from Concepción in the direction of the sea. There he would find the people who were best disposed to receive the seed of the Gospel.

"So he started out, and after walking six or seven leagues on land between two very large rivers—the Piratiní and Yjuhí—toward the sea, or lands of the Ibicuití, he set up the Reduction of Nuestra Señora de la Candelaria in a very desirable spot for entry into Ibicuití. For it seemed that all the doorways to the conversion of these people were closed by every other route, either because of the stubbornness of the Indians or the great distance of these Reductions by river. For from the Reduction de los Reyes at the entrance of the Ibicuití River, one had to go fifty leagues without seeing a single village; whereas this way, going from one Reduction to another, one could quickly reach the Ibicuití."

Vázquez Trujillo describes the organization of the Reductions of the Uruguay which Roque set up when he was superior.

He placed Pedro Romero in charge of the new Candelaria because of his vast experience. Andrés de la Rúa, a younger Spaniard who had made his studies in America, was stationed in Los Reyes. Miguel de Ampuero went to the Reduction of Javier; Diego de Alfaro and Tomás de Ureña went to Concepción, and Alfonso de Aragona and Juan del Castillo went to Piratiní.

Here we meet, for the first time, the name of Juan del Castillo, one of Roque's two companions destined to share his martyrdom and beatification.

MARTYRDOM

Juan del Castillo and
Alonso Rodríguez

UAN DEL CASTILLO was born in Belmonte, Cuenca, Spain on September 14, 1596, of distinguished, well-to-do parents, Alonso del Castillo and María Rodriguez. He entered the University of Alcalá to study law, and a year later he entered the Society of Jesus on March 21, 1614.

After his novitiate he was sent to the college of Huete for further study. When Father Juan de Viana, procurator of Paraguay, spoke at the college, young Juan felt inspired to volunteer for the mission and was accepted.

The group recruited by Juan Viana was impressive indeed; it included the martyrs Juan del Castillo and Alonso Rodríguez, as well as other missioners of notable stature, like Andreas Feldmann, Claude Royer, Pedro Comentale, and other young men from several different European nations. They all sailed on November 2, 1616, and reached Buenos Aires three and a half months later on February 15, 1617.

From Buenos Aires they set out for the *Colegio Máximo*, the Jesuit major seminary in Córdoba, to complete their philosophical studies. Documents from 1620 indicate that Juan del Castillo was teaching at that time in the college of Concepción, Chile. His contemporaries admired "his very humane manners" and his success as a teacher of young men.

At the end of this period of teaching, which is commonly known among Jesuits as "regency," Juan returned to Córdoba for theology studies, the final stage of his priestly preparation. He was ordained in November of 1625, though we do not know the precise date or the name of the ordaining bishop. In 1626 he was at work with the Indians.

Father Ferrufino states that "Juan del Castillo was stationed in San Nicolás, teaching the newly converted Indians with great effectiveness. His health, however, was quite frail; he became ill and only a strict order could persuade him to convalesce a bit. After a recovery he went back to work, preferring to use whatever strength he had in mission work rather than in leisurely retirement."

Ferrufino also tells us that "Father Roque chose Juan for the new Reduction, and thus the two missioners set out to take possession of it in the name of Jesus Christ." One could hardly imagine a more total contrast than that between the two future martyrs: Roque was strong and robust, Juan delicate and even sickly; yet they were alike in apostolic determination.

The new Reduction, founded on August 15, the feast of the Assumption, was naturally called "Asunción." Ferrufino adds: "What Juan del Castillo suffered can hardly be imagined, as he worked amid people unaccustomed not only to the precepts of the Gospel but even to human laws; he was alone, with no friends, with no consolation."

His short life as a missioner already seemed a martyrdom.

Alonso Rodríguez was born in Zamora, Spain, March 10, 1598, and entered the Jesuit novitiate of Villagarcía on March 24, 1614. He had just turned sixteen. His contemporaries speak of him as lively in temperament and alert in mind, and his professors judged him to be academically outstanding. They showed their esteem by selecting him to make a "solemn defense" in theology, an academic distinction reserved only for the very best students.

Alonso arrived in Buenos Aires on the Viana expedition and went with Juan del Castillo and others to continue their seminary training in Córdoba. While we have no clear documentation to support the opinion, Alonso may have been ordained a priest toward the end of 1623 or at the beginning of 1624. In evaluations made by his superiors and professors, he was rated "outstanding."

In 1626 Alonso Rodríguez went back to the novitiate to begin a sort of second noviceship following ordination. In Jesuit jargon this is called "the third probation" or "tertianship." Mastrilli Durán writes that Alonso "went to complete this training among the Guaycurús, the most difficult mission, and has already begun to preach in that language. In fact, he is the first priest to begin to overcome its difficulty, it being the most difficult language in the world." While Mastrilli Durán's judgment about the Guaycurú language is hardly scientific, we recall that that language proved impossible to Roque who was born in Paraguay and had spoken Guaraní from his childhood. Yet, languages of peoples living in adjacent lands often have nothing in common—one thinks of Hungarian and Rumanian, Finnish and Russian, Basque and Spanish, to mention only a few.

In 1628 Roque met Alonso in Itapúa. They went together to help found the new mission of Caaró. There Alonso was to share with Roque the last days of his short life.

Toward Caaró

ABOUT the end of October, 1628, Roque and Alonso set out for the new site of Caaró; it was located in the modern State of Rio Grande do Sul, Brazil. "On the first of November Roque raised the cross, baptized three children, and named the future Reduction *Todos los Santos* ["All Saints," the feast of the day].

"From that moment until the 15th of the month, the caciques of the region held a reunion to get to know the fathers and to receive the metal wedges, which they were very fond of. This constituted a sort of pledge that they would join the Reduction. If they decided otherwise, they were to return the gift." We are following a letter from the new provincial, Vázquez Trujillo. He goes on:

One had to praise Our Lord when observing the growth of this Reduction. The two fathers were particularly happy when, on the same day, after distributing 200 wedges before Mass, Father Roque wrote a note to Father Pedro Romero —in fact, the last he was to write in this life.

In this note he stated that the new Reduction was everything he could hope for, and that if he had more wedges some 500 more Indians would have come. In any case, there were already spiritual fruits, since three children were brought for baptism. The Reduction of Yjuhí also met the same success, since the Indians brought many children to Father Juan del Castillo for him to baptize.

Meanwhile, however, the principal cacique of Yjuhí, Ñezú, was already planning to kill Roque and his companions. There is a substantial amount of documentation available on the three deaths, and the historian José María Blanco has woven the pieces together in what seems a likely sequence.

As soon as he learned of Roque's death, the leading cacique of Concepción, Santiago Guarecupí, set out with his Indians together with a captain, Manuel Cabral, and gave this account of the plot:

The witch doctors [or shamans] who reckoned themselves gods among these Indians had a mortal hatred for the fathers, since they prevented them from being adored and deprived them of their many women and carnal vices. And since what the fathers preached was contrary to their wicked customs, they replied that it was not good to abandon the way of life of their forefathers, and that the god that they knew was the true god, instead of the one that the fathers preached, who was the god of the Spaniards and no more. For this reason they always tried to prevent the spread of the Gospel teaching.

One Indian witch doctor named Ñezú, who was considered a god and whom the other Indians greatly feared—both caciques and other witch doctors —held a meeting in the town of Yjuhí where Father Castillo was teaching the Indians. There he told the other Indians that it was right to kill all those fathers and burn their churches built in the Uruguay area, and destroy the crosses and images that they had brought; and those who had been baptized should return to their ancient way of life, since he willed and ordered it.

And to show them the way to undo the baptism, Ñezú called some of the baptized children and with water that he took from underneath himself, saying that it was sweat and a liquid distilled from his body, he washed their heads, chests, and shoulders, and scraped their tongues, saying that in doing so he was undoing their baptism, and he would do the same to all the other Christians of the area. Then he gave gentile names to the children, saying, "This is our perfect law, and not the one that those fathers teach."

He further ordered them to get ready to carry out whatever he commanded, which was to kill all the fathers and destroy the Christian name in that whole province. He asserted that they should not be afraid. That he, as the god that he was, would favor them and cast deep darkness on those who wanted to defend the fathers, and he would send jaguars to devour them and would send a deluge to drown them, and would raise hills over their towns, and would rise up to heaven and turn the land upside down. The Indians, who were very much afraid of him, believed him.

While Roque was working on the construction of a belfry, two Indians named Guarerá and Mbarú arrived from Yjuhí. They had orders from Ñezú "to have the cacique Caarupé kill Fathers Roque González de Santa Cruz and Alonso Rodríguez, so that we may retain our way of life and ancient songs."

The cacique Caarupé, accompanied by his slave Maranguá, was present at the construction of the belfry. A Paraná boy was punching holes in the timber to fit the bell onto it, and Roque was bent over to tie the bell clapper. When the slave saw Roque in that position, before he could even look up at them, at a signal from Caarupé the slave dealt such a blow to Roque's head with an *itaizá* [stone hatchet] that he died instantly.

A Paraná youth then dashed over to Alonso Rodríguez, who was coming out of the church where he had just said Mass, and told him what had happened. Alonso cried out: "What are you doing, my sons?" At that moment they crushed his skull with *itaizá* blows, dragging him dead to the church door.

The Indians then went back to Roque's body and mangled his head and face with blow after blow. They tore off the priests' garments, and cutting Alonso's body in two at the waist, dragged both bodies into the church. After stealing or smashing the church furnishings, they set both the church and the priests' cabin on fire.

During the bedlam of those moments, at least one Christian Indian raised his voice in protest. He was an aged cacique, the father-in-law of Carobay, one of the first caciques converted in the Uruguay area. An *itaizá* blow choked him to death, an anonymous martyr.

In the meantime, two messengers from Caarupé set off for Yjuhí to inform Ñezú that this orders had been successfully carried out. Others left with Caarupé to kill the other Jesuits in the area as well.

The next day, those Indians who had participated in the slaughter came back to examine what remained. They later testified that they heard voices and clearly identified that of Roque. All the witnesses agreed that everybody present could even distinguish Roque's words: "Though you kill me, I do not die. My soul goes to heaven, and I will not be far from you but will return. The punishment will not be long in coming."

Maranguá confessed that, when he saw Roque's heart, which had not burned, he concluded that the words of Roque came from his heart. He thereupon pierced it with an arrow and threw it back into the flames.

157

Meanwhile, Ñezú was informed of what had happened in Caaró. He set out from the forest dressed in a cape of feathers, and appeared among his people. He then ordered them to kill Juan del Castillo, as Roque and Alonso had been done away with. We have the following sworn testimony of an eyewitness, Pablo Arayú:

> Father Juan had just given wedges, fish hooks, and brooches to a cacique called Chetihagué together with his people, and he was registering their names. An elderly cacique named Quaraibí, a witch doctor, who carried a sword hidden under his leather garment, ordered a cacique named Araguirá to attack the father. This man grabbed Juan from behind and held his arms. Others then joined in the scuffle and they dragged Juan to the forest. There they began to tear off his clothes, leaving only a single sock, and the sleeves on his arms.
>
> An Indian called Mirungá then threw Juan to the ground, tied his wrists with ropes, and dragged him through the woods. This dislocated his arm. At this point, Tacandá, a slave of Ñezú, struck him in the belly with a heavy stone. They then dragged him lacerated and bloody, over stones and logs into a quagmire, where they crushed his head with a large stone. This killed

158

him. They left his body there for a while and rested. Then they dragged the body to another place and burned it. After grinding some of his bones they said, "Let the jaguars come and devour him!"

When asked what Father Juan had said and done while he was being dragged and killed, the witness replied: "He asked: My sons, what are you doing? His arms were so tightly fastened that he could only move his head from side to side. He said more, but with all the noise I couldn't make it out. In the forest, as they were dragging him, I heard him say "O Jesus!" and some other words in his own language, which I couldn't understand."

When asked why the Indians of Yjuhí killed Juan del Castillo, the witness replied that the witch doctor Ñezú had sent two Indians, Guarerá and Mbarú, to Caaró to the cacique Caarupé and ordered him to kill fathers Roque and Alonso, so that we could preserve our way of life and ancient songs.

Vázquez Trujillo tells what happened back in Candelaria on the Thursday after Roque's death. The young Indian from Concepción who fled toward Candelaria with the news "arrived the next day at nine in the morning where Father Pedro Romero was stationed. He was so troubled and nervous that it was clear that something terrible had happened. Father Romero, without even waiting to hear him speak, asked him for the message he was carrying. Now a bit calmer, the boy answered that he had no message, but was fleeing after seeing the Caaró Indians in a tumult and that, as far as he understood, they had laid hands on Father Roque.

Father Romero could not believe what he heard. He kept asking over and over, until he realized that what he had heard was true. He asked if the Indians had spoken with Roque or seen his face. For he believed that Roque was so eloquent and his countenance so venerable that they would not dare to do anything so evil.

Pedro Romero decided to send the boy and two other Indians to Piratiní and Yjuhí to let them know what had happened. But his friends urged him not to do this, so as not to agitate the whole territory. It would be better, they felt, to send two reliable men to Caaró to find out in secret what had really happened and whether the fathers were still alive and in need of help. If so, they and their families would go to assist them and notify the other Reductions.

This seemed to Father Romero to be the best

plan. So he sent two men exactly as suggested. Meanwhile Father Romero and all the people waited in deep anxiety.

The Indians had scarcely left when they spotted two other men on horseback coming from the direction of Caaró. For the moment they were overjoyed, believing, as they wanted to, that these were Roque and his companion.

But their relief did not last. They soon recognized the two boys from the Paraná. Father Romero asked: 'My sons, where are your fathers?' The young men sobbed and answered: 'We have no fathers now, they've been killed!'

The bad news stirred Father Romero into action. He sent messengers immediately to warn the fathers in the other Reductions.

The next day, Friday, some two hundred non-Christian Indians but with Christian hearts, started out for Caaró to collect the ashes of the saints. This they did so well that it could not have been better done if one of us had gone with them.

Separating the remains, they placed them on clean sheets that they had brought with them, and those bones that could not be identified were placed in a pillowcase. This is how they showed their devotion toward men they regarded as saints. When Father Romero asked if they did not feel nauseated doing this, they replied: 'How could we? They are our fathers!'

They gathered the relics and lined up in

double file with bows and arrows. They then carried the relics back unharmed; even the people of Caaró did not dare to attack them. Though they were watching and even followed them almost to Candelaria to see if they could catch them off guard with their treasure.

Scarcely had they crossed the arroyo when they heard men and women crying, young and old, piteous enough to break one's heart. As they reached the church door, so many people had gathered there to mourn the fathers that Father Romero himself had to leave and go to his house weeping as much as anyone.

Despite the enormous distances, news of the three deaths—especially that of Roque, since he was the best known—spread swiftly in all directions. Indians from other Reductions sped to Concepción by the hundreds offering to defend the missioners and the Christian Indians from further attacks. In fact, there is lengthy documentation about the time immediately following the martyrdom.

Of the several letters that we possess, that which Pedro Romero wrote to Governor Hernandarias and sent on to Vázquez Trujillo, is perhaps the most complete. He starts by apologizing for any delay in writing, given the rush of events at the time "of the death of our holy martyrs." Whether Romero was the first to refer to Roque, Alonso, and Juan as martyrs, we do not know; but the expression quickly became commonplace. Romero's letter goes on:

> First of all I must say that this gift sent by Our Lord in the death of our Saints cannot be attributed to haste or imprudence or lack of experience or any other cause that human reason looks for to avoid attributing to Our Lord what is truly his own. For divine Providence always cares for its servants, the preachers of the Gospel, like the holy Father Roque González and his two companions.
>
> It is certain that the present opportunities and the disposition that Our Lord places in souls to ask for the bread of God's word persuade us to share it without delay so that the Indians will not perish without it. For they cost our most sweet Redeemer so much. It was thanks to His

163

death and the work of His holy Apostles that
the world has not been lost, nor the faith ended.
Rather with the flowing of his precious
Blood the faith increases more and more. And
so we promise ourselves that with the blood of
our holy martyrs this new Christian society shall
grow great and bring forth abundant fruit. And
you will surely see from my account here that
this must be attributed to the Providence of Our
Lord.

This outburst of Pedro Romero, impet-
uous and overflowing with admiration for
his brother missioners, would one day seem
prophetic. For seventeen years later, on
March 22, 1645, he too would give his life
after being, like Roque, the superior of the
same Guaraní missions.

At the end of his letter Romero adds:
"After writing this I received a letter from
Father Marciel de Lorenzana written from
Asunción on December 23. It states: 'Little
is going on here, and we have little news
from where you are. I suppose you already
know about the glorious deaths of the holy
Fathers Roque González de Santa Cruz,

Alonso Rodríguez, and Juan del Castillo, who have so honored our province with their blood, and sancitified and fertilized that mission. The bishop was informed, and he saw fit to order a solemn thanksgiving service. And so on Saturday after the First Sunday of Advent the bells of the cathedral rang out and were followed by all the bells of the city. In our church a *Te Deum* was sung with great solemnity, together with all ornaments and a great number of candles."

While this festivity may strike the modern secular mind as a bit insensitive if not actually morbid, it seemed altogether fitting to Roque's contemporaries. While he was still living, Roque was widely regarded as a saint; and it is very likely that even if he had died a less dramatic death the occasion would have been celebrated as a moment of triumph for "their saint"; hence, in a way, his triumph was their triumph.

In baroque Europe the death of anyone venerated as a saint occasioned a great outpouring of glory and celebration, a sort of earthly reflection of the heavenly glory now surrounding Christ's faithful witness who now shared His victory. In any case, it is interesting that Roque's, last moments were celebrated at all levels of Paraguayan society, from the Guaranís living in the Reductions to the creole upper crust. This was true in spite of Roque's consistent struggle against much of what the latter stood for.

After going through the hundreds of pages of arguments brought for or against Roque's beatification during the official investigations, one discovers that the only serious doubt had to do not with his "heroic virtues," but with the precise motives of his assassins. The Promotor of the Faith, Salvator Natucci, did not question Roque's holiness, but whether he could be called, in the strictest sense, a "martyr." He adduced lengthy, sometimes subtle arguments to the effect that Roque died for other reasons: because he was a Spaniard rather than a witness of Christ; or that at least there was a mixture of cultural with the religious reasons for his death. The argument is worth taking seriously, and we will deal with it accordingly in our last chapter.

One who reads the documents of that period today is impressed by the admiration Roque received from his acquaintances and longtime associates. A few days before his own death, Luis de Bolaños, the Franciscan apostle to the Guaranís, solemnly declared under oath that Roque "always persevered in the highest form of virtue and holiness" and that "in accord with his good life, virtue, and customs, as well as his apostolic work and the conversion of souls which distinguished his life up to the moment when he was killed, this witness judges him to be a true martyr." Similar testimonies are repeated again and again throughout the official "process," which, as we have noted, began just a few weeks after Roque's death and that of his companions.

In the city of Corrientes, Argentina, in 1630, another "ordinary process" took place which was equally impressive in its evaluation of the life and work of Roque and his companions. One of the testimonies was given by the captain and lieutenant governor Manuel Cabral. Cabral asserted under oath that he know Roque well and had observed "how much labor, hunger, cold, mosquitoes, and other hardships he had undergone, such as no one could have endured except a saint, a truly apostolic man. This witness knows many details about how he constantly risked his life for the love and service of Our Lord, and how he endangered his life every day for the good of souls. And not only the Indians in the Uruguay province loved Father Roque for his holiness, example, and charity, but also all the other Indians throughout the whole Paraná region as well." This testimony comes from a man who was very much involved in things of this world.

On the other hand, a more private testimony, to which we now have access, may, paradoxically, be even more reliable. It comes from the unemotional, objective evaluations made from time to time by every individual Jesuit's religious superiors. While these are normally confidential, they become in time more generally accessible to historians. This happened especially at the time of the suppression of the Society of Jesus. After the suppression private documents were often requisitioned by governments and either sold or otherwise made public.

In Roque's case, the superior general in Rome, Muzio Vitelleschi, wrote a confidential letter to the provicial superior in Paraguay, which is included in the documents and may surprise many readers. He states: "They say that Father Roque González, who is working in the Paraná area, is an expert in the Guaraní language. But he is scrupulous and not affable and gives his companions a less pleasant impression. I mention this so that you will make two requests of him: one, that he treat others more gently and affably; the other, that he teach the language to his companions." The letter is dated April 20, 1620.

Personally I was delighted to find this among the many documents available. While all the other appraisals given by his fellow Jesuits are quite positive (even though they admit his tendency toward scrupulousness and a certain "melancholic" character, in the terminology of the period), we discover that Roque's strength did not always strike his peers as unflawed. One might suggest that he had some of the "faults of his virtues." At this period of his life, in any event, he may have asked as much of others as he did of himself. Furthermore, he may not have been a good teacher of Guaraní, since it was a native language to him. And even after the bad experience of failing to learn Guayacurú, he may not have realized how enormously difficult Guaraní is to anyone trained only in European languages.

Whether or not Roque was able to correct these faults, we can only guess. Surely he must have made an effort. In any case, we have another evaluation—the last written before his death—by the local provincial Nicolás Mastrilli Durán who personally worked with him: "Roque González, great missioner and 'conquistador' of souls; a great religious man, humble, quite zealous in his work with the Indians; highly esteemed, even among the pagans; among Spaniards some cultural lack [*falta la opinión de letras*]. It would be a terrible shame if he is ever removed from mission work among the pagans."

Written shortly before Roque's death in the uninflated style of an official evaluation, this concise résumé of Roque's personality impresses us, in hindsight, more than any florid encomium done in the rhetoric of the time.

The Roque Legend

GARLANDS of legends often accumulate around the lives of national heroes—a Washington, a Lincoln, a Napoleon—even during their time on earth. The same thing, of course, also happens to saints, not only medieval ones like Patrick, Boniface, and Francis of Assisi, but also more modern saints like Philip Neri or Francis Xavier. The careful historian often dedicates years to finding the real person, as did the late Georg Schurhammer, who dedicated some sixty years and 343 articles and books to disentangle Francis Xavier from forests of myth.

It is not surprising that Roque, a person of possibly comparable stature, should inspire a sort of minor mythology, especially after such a dramatic death. Roque's martyrdom should not have astonished anyone, least of all his fellow martyr Pedro Romero. And yet we have seen that Pedro found it hard to believe that Roque had actually been killed.

The Indians who had taken part in Roque's murder immediately reported the amazing story that they had heard his voice and that the voice came from his heart, the only part of his body to survive the fire which they themselves had set. At this point it is impossible to know what motivated their story or to grasp its full import. Besides, although the core of their testimony is the same, minor discrepancies in the accounts given by Caarupé, Maranguá, and others, give us pause.

What makes the episode peculiarly interesting, however, is the concrete evidence of Roque's heart which is preserved in the Chapel of the Martyrs in Asunción. Is it really Roque's heart or not? Documents assure us that the heart of Roque González was authenticated by the Jesuit provincial Juan Bautista Ferrufino and sent to Rome with his official seal on October 16, 1634. During the years when the Society was suppressed from 1773 to 1814, the heart was kept in the little chapel of St. Ignatius in the Gesù church in Rome. In 1928 it was given a thorough medical examination by Dr. Osvaldo Zacchi in Rome, who submitted the following report:

> After a simple external morphological examination, it can be affirmed with absolute certainty that this is a human heart, very well preserved in a state of desiccation.

After giving a number of technical medical details, Dr. Zacchi concludes:

> In the wall of the righ ventricle one observes a perforation, approximately five millimeters large, clean and in a perfectly straight line, about four centimeters long, the outlets of which appear as follows: one near the right limit of the heart, the other two fingers' wide near the left. Examining the whole, which is absolutely open, one sees that it is included in the thickness of the miocardium without touching the corresponding ventricular cavity. I judge that this perforation was produced by an outside body, penetrating, pointed (an awl or an arrow), which remained there a considerable time.

All of this matches what we know of Roque's heart being pierced by an arrow.

In 1928 after Zacchi's examination, the relic was transferred to Buenos Aires. There, in the Colegio del Salvador, other studies were made by doctors. In 1968, thanks to the suggestion of Pedro Arrupe, the Jesuit superior general, the relic was finally brought to Asunción. When I first saw it in 1976, it was kept in a small chapel in the Paraguayan

174

provincial's residence; but that same year it was fittingly placed in the Chapel of the Martyrs in commemoration of the 400th anniversary of Roque's birth.

Another episode in the Roque González tradition, while less tangible, is certainly charming. His colleague, Ruiz de Montoya, after dedicating several chapters of his *Conquista Espiritual* to Roque's work, tells this story in Chapter 59:

> One of the accomplices in the martyrdom of these saints [Roque, Alonso, and Juan] was a famous cacique named Tambavé, who took as spoils from his inhuman deed a horse on which the venerable Father Roque used to ride. The horse, showing his feelings in the absence of his master, refused to eat, even when they offered him hay and grain. The Indians kept on offering the food, suspecting that he was refusing from grief and mourning. The horse went about the camp to the huts where the Indians were celebrating the deaths of the saints, with tumult and games and the smell of wine. As though giving a speech, the horse neighed fiercely. The Indians went out to see him, and persuaded by the animal's perseverance, they admitted that he did it from grief. This was further confirmed by another fact: that the horse never again allowed

any Indian to mount him. One of them put on the father's cassock and pretending to be the horse's holy master, was able to restrain him and even mounted him. But the horse still refused to eat and grew very thin. The Indians saw that he would be of no use to them, and though admonished by the animal, they killed him.

Montoya adds a touching detail:

And if this was a testimony to the glory of the martyrs, even greater testimony was given by the conversion of the murderers, who attained heaven thanks to Roque's prayers. For many Indians repented and confessed their brazen deeds with sorrow. I will only add that the Indian named Tambavé changed from being a cacique and lord to being the fathers' helper. He assisted them in their works of charity with the sick, serving with much love, and in other lowly tasks as well. So great was his conversion, that like another St. Paul, he helped in the conversion of many gentiles who today enjoy baptism and the Christian faith.

A third item—hardly less curious but more scientifically documented—is not legendary. I know of it through the research done by the English historian Herbert Thurston, a man of flawless credentials as a critical investigator. Indeed Thurston's reputation as an iconoclastic hagiographer was such as to gain him the sobriquet of Devil's Advocate *par excellence*. He reports and documents the following series of events that happened in the United States toward the middle of the nineteenth century.

Two well-known intellectuals, Thomas Low Nichols and his wife Mary Sargeant Neal Gove (whose lives are included in the *Dictionary of American Biography*) were much involved in the spiritist movement of the mid-century. One day they visited Archbishop John Purcell of Cincinnati and told him their strange story. They had received several mystifying visions; one that particularly troubled them was that of a figure dressed in a black cassock with blood-stained cincture, who announced that he was a Jesuit. They hardly knew anything about Jesuits, knew no Catholics personally, and had

177

no idea where to turn. Later on, the same figure appeared to them and blamed them for not investigating his appearance. He gave his name as "González." It was then that they approached Archbishop Purcell, who sent them to see Father Maurice Oakley, the rector of the small Jesuit school in Cincinnati named Xavier, which is today the large university with the same name.

Before they could meet Oakley, however, another vision took place, this time of a Jesuit who gave his name as "Ignacio de Loyola." He offered certain "rules for regulating their lives" (apparently something from the Spiritual Exercises). Then they had a fourth vision of someone called "Francisco Xavier," who proceeded to instruct them about the Catholic religion.

When Dr. and Mrs. Nichols finally met Father Oakley, he was as perplexed by their story as Archbishop Purcell had been, particularly at their knowledge of Catholic teaching, which even included the recently defined doctrine of the Immaculate Conception (1854). They assured Oakley that they had not done any reading whatsoever on any of these subjects. Thereupon they asked to be received into the Church. Satisfied that they were already thoroughly instructed in the faith, Oakley complied with their wish. The Nichols then wrote a full account of their conversion, attributing it in the first place to Roque González.

This entire bizarre story is peculiar even in hagiography. What seems to authenticate it, however, is the quality of the persons involved, all well-known in the last century. The Nichols were personal friends of other intellectuals of the time, such as John Ruskin, Thomas Carlyle, Ralph Waldo Emerson, Horace Greeley, and Edgar Allen Poe. Poe, in fact, includes Mary Gove (Mrs. Nichols) in his work *The Literati*, calling her "a very interesting woman," and with male superiority, he praises her literary style as "quite remarkable for its luminousness and precision, two qualities very rare with her sex"!

We are thus confronted here, not with

tales lost in a misty past, but with a report written by scholarly people with the skeptical background of the last century.

Roque González, Martyr

THE TERM *MARTYR* is hardly in vogue today; it smacks a bit of naïveté. Further, like many once awesome words—*genocide*, for example—it has been so inflated by overuse that it has lost any precise meaning. What is even worse, given the fad for psychiatric jargon, it suggests something rather less, not more, than normal. Teenagers sometimes taunt their peers for having a "martyr complex," meaning they have some kind of mental aberration or morbidity.

Revisionist historians, too, have added their bit to the devaluation of the term *martyr*. They insist quite rightly on the need to examine both sides and not judge everything or everyone in facile black-and-white categories. Today, for example, we are becoming aware that few wars were totally justified on one side and totally malicious on the other. Four decades after World War II few independent historians see even that catastrophe exclusively in terms of Nazi iniquity, as though all the evil were the responsibility of a single side. We have been taught to remember Dresden, too.

At the same time thorough scholarship does not necessarily diminish historical characters. It was heartening, for example, to learn that a recent questionnaire answered by more than a thousand United States historians resulted in an amazing near-unanimity in evaluations of the better-known United States presidents. Despite probing studies of every facet of Abraham Lincoln's public and private life, for example, these historians, regardless of regional background, almost unanimously recognized him as the greatest president in the country's history. Despite human limitations and foibles, some famous personalities still stand out as authentically great.

Among such people, those who are officially declared to be "saints" or "blesseds" surely hold a special place: for they have had to pass the scrutiny of Devil's Advocates, at least for the past several centuries. Ever since Pope Benedict XIV tightened the requirements for canonization in the eighteenth century, the tests have been as probing as any scholar could wish for. The "Defender of the Faith" is charged with the serious responsibility of discovering any and every facet of the candidate's life that might call canonization into question. Anyone who has examined such "processes" with their hundreds of documents knows that neither enthusiasm nor even popular acclaim can have a decisive vote. Saints are not declared so by referendum or by popular acclaim.

In the case of Roque González de Santa Cruz, we have easy access to some thousand pages of documents published in 1932 and available in most major libraries. So we can observe the painstaking procedures of the Roman congregation which is entrusted with examining the life and death of a possible saint. To be sure, the volume includes panegyrics as well as criticisms; and while the biographer uses both, he tries to evaluate and demythologize in a careful way.

We have already seen the defense of his actions which was offered by the shaman Ñezú. The same sort of argument is eloquently presented by another Indian leader, Potiravá, who hated what he saw as colonial oppression in the work of the missioners. The documents offer this eloquent précis of Potiravá's case; to be sure, it would have been even more eloquent in the original Guaraní.

I feel that neither I nor you have committed any offense; the harm is what these strangers from another land are doing to our way of life and the ancient customs of our forefathers.

What was our heritage except our freedom? The same nature that freed us from the burden of being slaves to others—did it not also free us from being tied down to one place for any longer than our free choice decided?

Wasn't all this land around us our common inheritance, without our having to be in the valley more than in the woods?

Why do we need this masked slavery of the

Reductions to subject us, or worse yet, to subject our children?

Aren't you afraid that these men who call themselves 'fathers' are saying this to disguise their ambition and are really making slaves of those they call their 'dear sons'?

Do we need any more examples in Paraguay of what the Spaniards really are, when we see their promises held out as bait?

Neither our humiliation will remedy their pride, nor our obedience their ambition. All they want is their own wealth and the misery of others.

Have you any doubt that those who are introducing unknown gods today will tomorrow, with the hidden power that is given to control others, impose new laws or shamelessly sell us into another captivity as punishment for our being so blind as to believe them?

Those who are so anxious to deprive you of the women you enjoy, why do they presume to do this, except that they desire the same prey that they are taking away from you?

Why do they do this except for their own whim; why do they deprive you of raising a large family?

And most of all, don't you feel the outrage toward your gods when a foreign, hateful law takes away what we received from our ancestors —a law that takes away our divine oracles,

substituting for our true gods the worship of a
wooden beam? [the cross]

Can we let a foreign lie overcome the truth
of our fathers? This threat menaces all of us. But
the blow will fall hardest on you if you don't
stop these treacherous tyrants by killing them.
By putting up with them, you will be forging
your own iron cages!

It is not surprising that the Devil's Advocate in Roque's case, Salvator Natucci,
made a great deal of this objection: that the
death of Roque and his companions was
brought about for reasons that were really
sociopolitical and only superficially religious
(in the official Latin text, *specie tenus fuit religiosum, reapse vero politicum*).

From the viewpoint of those Indians
who did not accept Christianity, one can
hardly doubt that they killed Roque and his
companions for what we would call broadly
cultural reasons. For they did not distinguish
between the specifically religious and the sociopolitical.

Yet when we call Roque, Alonso, and
Juan martyrs, we should not identify their

personal motivation with that of their killers. In such cases, both killer and victim can well be equally sincere. The one kills to save his way of life, his culture, his very being. The other dies to give witness to Christ; the word *martyr* means precisely witness.

In the long history of Christian martyrs, this distinction must be respected in most, if not all, cases. As we can see from the correspondence between Pliny the Younger and the Roman emperor Trajan, neither relished killing Christians, but they felt that the law must be carried out, since Christians stubbornly (as they put it) refused to perform what they saw as certain cultural-religious rites which, to the Christians, meant idolatry. When Queen Elizabeth I of England ordered the death of Edmund Campion, Robert Southwell, and other Catholic martyrs, her motivation could well have been quite sincerely political, for "reasons of state." Nonetheless, by canonizing such people the Church judges them to be witnesses of the Faith, and thus to Christ. It is neither charitable nor necessary to pass judgment on all

186

those who kill martyrs as though we thought them insincere. When we declare a person a martyr, without judging the executioners' motivation, we simply mean that such a person's life and death is a witness, authentic and even heroic.

In the case of Roque González, a special irony comes to mind. When the Indians slew Roque, they were killing the creole who had fought most strenuously for their own human rights. We recall how he defended the rights of the Indians even against his own elder brother. As Roque saw it, the system of Reductions was the best, if not the only instrument for saving the Indians from the Spaniards and creoles, his own relatives.

At the same time, it is hard for us to imagine the degree of suspicion and hatred felt by the Indians toward the Spaniards, Portuguese, and creoles. A century and a half later, another great missionary, Martin Dobrizhoffer, S.J., when writing his *History of the Abipons*, quotes a cacique named Roy who "admitted sincerely to me that he and his people put no trust in any Spaniard or

Portuguese, not the slightest credence in their words or assurances of friendship. To win over his confidence and good will, I repeatedly assured him that I was neither Portuguese nor Spanish. To illustrate this and to assure him all the more, I explained that between my native country [Czechoslovakia] and Spain or Portugal there lay many countries and seas; that my parents, grandparents, and greatgrandparents did not understand a single word of Spanish. After I explained this in all sincerity, he immediately informed his people that I was neither a Spaniard nor a Portuguese. This helped immensely in establishing between us the bonds of friendship and good will" (Vol. 1, pp. 171-72).

If this was the attitude of Indians who lived more than a century after Roque's death, it is no wonder that Ñezú and others conspired to kill him at the very time the Conquest was still going on in that remote region of Paraguay. To them, regardless of all he had done and was doing, Roque was a symbol of the hated Spaniard (or Portuguese) and the enemy of their people. What is surprising is that so many thousands of Indians did trust Roque and the other missioners, despite their European or creole nationalities.

Roque, Alonso, and Juan and the twenty-three other Jesuits who died violent deaths as missioners in Paraguay were not killed by "their own" Indians, Indians from Reductions that had been fully settled, but by people who had not experienced, from within the system, the humane and Christian life that the Reductions made possible. The most palpable proof of the affection felt by Reduction Indians toward the missioners lies in the fact that they never killed "their own" missioners. Some, to be sure, did leave the Reductions in quest of their nomadic and traditional "way of life." But, though nothing could have been easier to do, these Reduction Indians never killed a single Jesuit.

Whatever the motives of Roque's killers, he and his companions died as witnesses to their faith. Furthermore, their deaths, swift for Roque and Alonso, somewhat more protracted for Juan, were simply the consummation of years of self-oblation freely and knowingly undertaken.

Bartomeu Meliá, a Spanish Jesuit anthropologist who has worked for years among various tribes and who possesses a rare grasp of the Indian mentality, has this to say about Roque's death:

> Roque died for his religion, his faith in Christ, and his love for Christ. The faith was preached by word of mouth in Guaraní and with the language of sacraments and other sacramental signs (baptism, matrimony, Mass, the cross, the church, processions, bells, and the like). The love was the love of one's neighbor, which translated into a new economy of more developed and more productive work, solid and more comfortable houses, adequate clothing, abundant and stable sources of food, and liberation from the abuses of witchcraft and the ultimate arbitrariness of the shamans.

For all of this the missioners died. But Meliá goes on to add an original interpretation that strikes me as both startling and challenging to all of us Christians of European descent: "Roque was killed by the priest-chieftains of the Guaraní religion and by the colonial system itself—those Spaniards who were *figuras de cristiano.* If his death was religiously related—and indeed it was—the principal culprit in Roque's martyrdom was the 'false' colonial religion"—the unchristian behavior of many so-called Christians.

NOTES

Note on the word Reduction

The term *reduction,* a transliteration of the Spanish *reducción,* has become standard in dictionaries and text books for mission settlements, especially for those in Latin America. Since a vast literature has been written about the missions directed by Jesuits, notably those in the Paraguay area, many readers identify the term exclusively with these Jesuit reductions of Paraguay.

While I find the word less than happy, since at least in its modern connotation it suggests some kind of diminishment, there seems no way to avoid it. In documents of the period, however, other happier synonyms abound: *pueblo, doctrina* (suggesting that the missions' main purpose was Christian instruction), or simply *misión.* Reductions existed in other parts of the Spanish empire, from Mexico to Peru and the Philippines, at the same time as those in Paraguay and even before.

What seems to make the Paraguay reductions better known and leads them to be thought of as *the* reductions may be their success and their long endurance, for some 160 years. They captivated the imaginations not only of young European Jesuits—some 14,000 of them volunteered for the arduous enterprise—but also of writers even in non-Catholic countries, some friendly, others hostile. Voltaire rid-

Conquistador without Sword

iculed the reductions in *Candide* and then praised
them enthusiastically in his *Essai sur les moeurs* as "in
some ways the triumph of humanity."

A recent English history of the reductions that
may be recommended is Philip Caraman's *The Lost
Paradise* (Seabury). My own volume, done in collaboration with José María Blanch, *Lost Cities of Paraguay*
(Loyola University Press), offers a rather complete
visual record of what remains of the reductions' art
and architecture and should be available in all good
libraries. It also explains the political structure of the
reductions as well as the causes of their abrupt dis-
establishment in 1767-68.

Note on the Encomienda *System*

Spanish law attempted to protect the rights of
Indians to their lands and it forbade the enslavement
of the Indians. At the same time, however, to attract
Spaniards to colonize America, large grants of land
were made to conquerors and colonists in a system
known as *encomienda*. The *encomendero* was to receive
payment in tribute and services from Indians in return
for protecting them and Christianizing them.

In practice, however, the system led to a kind of
feudalism, and the missionaries often condemned it
as actually a disguised form of slavery. Half a century
before Roque's struggle against the encomienda system, Bartolomé de las Casas and other missioners in
far-away Middle America were pressuring the Crown
to enact "new laws" to protect the Indians' rights

(1542). These laws, in fact, were enacted and forbade the granting of new encomiendas, took away rights from encomenderos who had abused their Indians, and provided that the encomiendas should cease upon the death of the encomenderos.

In a world-wide empire such as Spain's, with communications a matter of months from colonies to Spain and again from Spain to the colonies, these humane laws were generally unenforceable. Viceroys in far away Mexico City or Lima who tried to enforce laws in protection of the Indians faced rebellion or at least inertia on the part of many encomenderos. In fact, the encomiendas tended to be transformed into large family estates, and the Indians were often little better off than slaves.

In Roque's time Paraguay was under the viceroy of Lima, thousands of miles away, and the Indians had few to defend them except the missioners. The reductions became havens not only protecting the Indians from the slave-raiders from São Paulo, the *bandeirantes*, but also from the abuses of the encomendero system among native creoles. These people resented any restraint on their exploitation of the indigenous peoples.

While this book is explicitly about Roque González, I do not mean in any way to belittle the important work done previously on behalf of the Indians by other priests and bishops. As early as 1511, the Dominican Antonio de Montesinos, recently arrived from Spain, preached to the colonists like another John the Baptist: "You are all living in mortal sin, and you will live and die in sin because of the cruelty and tyranny with which you abuse these innocent people."

An even more famous Dominican, and later a bishop, Bartolomé de las Casas, was himself an encomendero; but recognizing the evils of the system, he turned over his Indians to the governor of Santo Domingo on August 15, 1514. Shortly thereafter he sailed back to Spain, where he persuaded Charles V to issue just laws in defense of the Indians and to grant the right to begin "villages of free Indians," communities that anticipated the Jesuit reductions by almost a century.

Between 1544 and 1568 a beautiful movement in defense of the Indians was led by a group of heroic bishops, almost all of the Dominicans, whom Enrique Dussel calls the Latin American Fathers of the Church. Indeed, Bishop Antonio de Valdivieso was stabbed to death in León, Nicaragua on February 26, 1550. He was martyred because of his love for and struggle on behalf of the Indians. One thinks of him as a precursor of Roque González and of today's Archbishop Oscar Romero.

What makes Roque's defense of the Indians exceptional, if not singular, is the fact that he was native-born and had to struggle against his own kinsmen in far-away Paraguay. The earlier "conquistadors without swords" were Spanish-born and were closer to the centers of power and to communications with the Spanish Crown.

APPENDIX

*Letter of Roque González de Santa Cruz to
his Brother Francisco in Asunción*

The grace of Our Lord be always with you.

I have received your letter and understand from
it and from other letters the strong feelings and complaints you have regarding the Indians and especially
the feelings you have against us.

This is nothing new, nor anything that started
yesterday. The *encomendero* gentlemen and soldiers
have long complained and even gone further by stir-
ring up strong opposition to the Society of Jesus. This,
in fact, is a great honor to us.

I say this because the cause of the Indians is so
just, and because they have and have had a right to
be free from the harsh slavery and forced labor called
personal service. Indeed, they are exempt from this by
natural law, divine and human.

These complaints grew even more serious after
members of the Society fulfilled their obligation as
faithful ministers of God Our Lord and vassals of his
majesty the King and supported what he ordered
most justly through his visitor: that the Indians
should be free from the servitude in which they were
kept. The Royal Audiencia (in spite of appeals) confirmed this, and the Indians understood the freedom
in which they were placed by our lord the King, and
they paid their tribute to him. The *encomendadores,*

197

however, were afraid that in supporting this we would do them harm.

The members of the Society were in these towns, "deceiving" (as they say) and preventing the Indians. The Indians then would agree to pay tribute to his Majesty because they did not want to be personal servants of the colonists as they had been before. To avoid all this they [the *encomendadores*] petitioned that we be expelled from here.

Meanwhile in Asunción things happened which I shall pass over in silence (I do not know where they happened) which you and the whole city witnessed, and things went so far that petitions were made to have us expelled from here by force and for soldiers to come here for that purpose. Someone even came, in consequence of these petitions, to throw us out of our church and keep us from saying Mass in it. To forestall this catastrophe, neither the justice of the Society was sufficient, nor the peaceful means taken by our Father Procurator, Diego de Torres, a person venerated for his holiness and learning not only in these kingdoms but also in Spain and Italy. Nor was your influence effective, true father of this commonwealth. And so this hostility increased.

But then the Indians stopped going to Mass with the colonists and preferred to pay tribute here as his Majesty had ordered them. For this, in the accusation of the residents of Paraguay, they had already risen up, or were on the point of doing so, since they were not going to serve. And the colonists blamed all of this entirely on the members of the Society of Jesus who were here.

But neither the Indians nor we ourselves—though we would have advised this—are at fault. Rather we have merit in the sight of God Our Lord and his majesty the King, who would be very happy if the Indians could know and use his justice; and (as I understand) he would appreciate this very much. And his Royal Council ordered through his visitor that the Indians not be expelled from our towns in order to perform *mita* [equivalent slavery].

All of this was confirmed by the Royal Audiencia of Chuquisaca, which ordered it to be observed as long as the Royal Council did not rule otherwise. The colonists have dared to expel the Indians from their own towns against justice and against the decrees that they should not go. Captain IU [*sic*] Ramos de Vera, who came for them, said this. And the Indians told him that they wanted to do what his Majesty ordered, they wanted to pay the tribute and tax owed to their *encomenderos* while they remained in their own lands; and they protested that they were going to Paraguay against their will. This reply was the cause of great grief among the Indians and ourselves.

It is clear to me that the facts are as I have described them. Besides, an *encomendero* in Asunción wrote to me that he felt great charity toward me, adding that if we changed our minds regarding the *tasa* and tributes, the *encomenderos* would be happy for us to be here and would give us whatever was necessary. From this, sir, you will see the reason for the complaints that they have, and the reason why the householders have tried to expel us from here. But over and above this, more is needed to satisfy their new complaints, since they have such hatred for Indians and for us; and they blame us for everything.

These complaints are based on three charges. First, that not as many Indians as they wanted have left this town to serve their *encomenderos* and other personnel. Secondly, the majority of those who did leave have returned here. And thirdly, because of this shortage of servants they themselves cannot carry out their intentions of serving God and his Majesty.

As to the first charge, the Indians, then as well as now, had no obligation to leave their lands. They invoked his Majesty's justice as he commanded through his visitor for its preservation. And Hernandarias, who came in his Majesty's name to declare this to the Indians (he being their protector) ordered them absolutely not to leave. And with regard to what you said about those obliged to pay tribute: they had no obligation other than to pay a tribute of five pesos. They did not have to leave their wives and children and go to serve the colonists in such far-away lands and for such a long time. But, nevertheless, since you ordered this and they were afraid of being forced to do it as you told us, we asked about thirty of them to do it to avoid other greater evils, and they were the only ones that you commanded.

Most of the Indians have returned to their towns, some here and others elsewhere. They gave as their reasons for returning the great labor, the bad treatment, and the lack of food. This last would be reason enough, since each person has to take care to preserve his life.

We have given no reason to say that we are the cause of this "problem," and we are not to be blamed. Rather, those who do so demonstrate clearly their bad will and the strong desire they have to harm the Society of Jesus. For before reaching this Reduction, the Indians had come from places where we were not stationed; and there were also Indians from Atica and even people from the Paraguay region. But the fault of the Indians from this Reduction is greater (as the *encomenderos* claim) than that of the other Indians who have fled only because we are here. And not satisfied with this, they further charged (as I am told) that the Indians whose caciques had made them return to our towns went back to call or persuade the others who had stayed; and they said that even you seemed inclined to believe this. But we are not two-faced, sir, and Diego Hernández, a person who has returned here, told me that the person who most recently stirred up the people was a *ladino* Indian from Itá.

Regarding the third complaint, that we obstructed those who intended to give service to God and the King, I reply first of all that this presupposes, in the language of the citizens and soldiers, that the Indians are the ones who do all the evil. But apart from this, what service of God Our Lord do the Indians prevent? God does not command the Gospel of Our Lord Jesus Christ to be preached with the noise of arms and with pillage. What He rather commands is the example of a good life and holy teaching. This is what the holy Apostles and apostolic men did, even going so far as to shed their blood. In fact, three holy men of our Society shed their blood for this cause in Chile. And if their intentions are what is reported among the soldiers—namely to pillage the Itatín Indians under the pretext that the father is settling them under the shelter of their arms—I do not believe this will please his Majesty. Rather he will see that this is contrary to the decree and command of his visitor. The only thing that I believe could be of service to his Majesty is, when mines are discovered, to advise whether they should be worked. And for this a dozen men and Indians would be enough. With only four men Captain Vallejos could have entered safely in search, and he would have saved himself many disputes and much grief. In this way the labor would have been proportionate to the result. But the expedition in question was calculated to punish those Indians that left. Those Indians now spend their own money to increase the patrimony of the King. For this his Majesty will certainly forgive their leaving the military service and he will be happy that they were in their own houses and did not come to afflict and trouble those other poor Indians who are also his vassals. For as I have said, without exhausting and wasting eighty soldiers, the purpose could have been achieved with a dozen, an account could have been given to his Majesty, and the Indians would have remained free.

Of the other charge made against the Indians; that if they did not go they would be disobedient to the royal court, his Majesty does not contradict himself. When he had ordered them so justly and in such a Christian way not to leave against their will, it was not wrong on their part to comply with justice by not leaving. Our King, being such a good Catholic, has the highest regard for the safety of his vassals and for the integrity of his royal conscience; and he wants his patrimony to be in accord with reason and justice without any harm to his vassals. In the Indies he commands that the Indians not be forced to leave their own environment, even if this means less work. This is clear from the decrees of his Royal Council, which were brought here some five or six years ago by the Procurator of Chuquisaca, who brought them from Spain. I heard him read them in full.

In accordance with these decrees, sir, the Indians cannot be forced to go, nor charged, nor punished as disobedient if they do not go, since they are not disobeying the orders or commands of the king our lord, but they are acting in conformity with them. And as long as there is no clear contrary command of his Majesty, no one can punish the Indians. Now if a certain number of Indians are going, it is against their wills and that of their chiefs; they are being forced by your threats even if they are not actually being punished.

To avoid these harms, we have asked that some Indians be sent, though others wished to appeal to justice, as I do. Although those that go will suffer now, Our Lord Who sees and knows all things will send a remedy. And finally, the day is not far off when God will reward service and good works and punish affronts, especially those done to the poor. I hope that you will see clearly that the householders and *encomenderos* have given false information about these people—perhaps they have been blinded by their passion—when they say that, though they observe the ordinances, they have no Indians to help them pay off the many years of tribute that they owe.

This has amazed me a great deal, because I know for certain how much wealth these people have, even if they appear in their shirtsleeves. Their wealth could never repay all they owe the Indians. And because the *encomenderos* live in such a state of blindness, no God-fearing priest will hear their confessions. For my part I tell you that I will not hear the confession of any one of them, for anything in this world, because they have done evil and are not willing to admit it, much less to make restitution and amend their lives. In the next world their eyes will be opened, to their great distress, unless they mend their ways now and make up with Indians in the sight of Him who is infinitely wise and cannot be deceived.

Now it would not be a bad thing in order to avoid such distress, for the *encomenderos* to do what Hernandarias did, settling everything and freeing the Indians from tribute for a good number of years. But since they do not wish to do this, let them not say that the Indians owe them money or service. You should not ask, after eighteen years of service, whether Andrés owes you anything. Or Martín who served seven continuous years in Asunción and came back yesterday. I am told that he was just married and had a farm for himself and his wife, and was taken and held here.

This you should have remedied. If my intention were to argue this point, I could fill this document with just complaints enough to break one's heart, and I could offer proof from the Indians who live here.

If you were to ask the people in this town before the Procurator if their *encomenderos* owe them anything, however small, he would return and the Indians would certainly demand payment for their work and their own lands. The visitor, since this is such a labyrinthine problem, turned this matter over to the fathers confessor and punished those who asked him for justice.

But suppose that the *encomenderos* get their tribute, without settling the matter or paying the Indians for what they owe them. The Indians want to work on their own land and pay themselves and plow their fields to support themselves and their wives and children. They will not be idle nor do little. You will only escape the anxiety you feel about the idleness of these Indians by taking measures that are completely contrary to their souls and bodies; this happens when they are separated from their wives. This is the spiritual and temporal ruin of these peoples; and as I have observed in particular cases, they become vagabonds in strange lands and byways, with no instruction whatsoever.

Conquistador without Sword

Through letters that I have received and in conversations with other persons, I know that there have been irresponsible and grievous complaints about the Society of Jesus and its sons. We who are, though unworthy, sons of the Society forgive them from our hearts for what they have done to us, and we lovingly beg Our Lord as the Father of Mercy to have mercy on them and forgive them.

It is true that the Divine Majesty is much offended by affronts against his priests and religious persons, and that he visits His divine justice on those malefactors with such horrible punishments that it makes one's flesh shudder to hear and read the accounts of those punishments in Holy Scripture. No one mocks God Our Lord, whose arm is all powerful. And I admit that I fear a grievous punishment from heaven in this province for the serious failures of its people. And now especially, they continue to provoke God's anger and fill the measure of His wrath by not allowing the fathers to work peacefully in the field.

May the Lord be praised for everything. He is worthy of all praise and glory. We are happy to be despised according to His will. May His Majesty give the grace for His will to be fulfilled in everything. And may he preserve you.

December 13, 1614

(Translation edited by George Lane, S.J.)

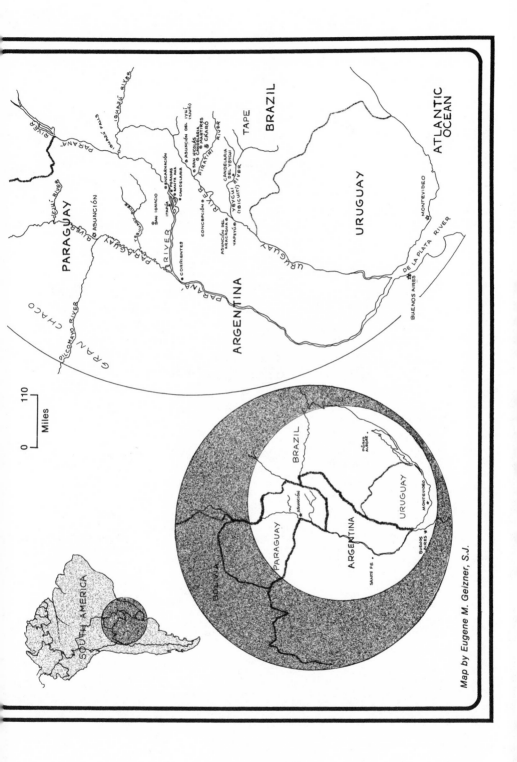

Map by Eugene M. Geizner, S.J.